Active Assessment for
Active Science

Active Assessment for Active Science

◆

A Guide for Elementary School Teachers

George E. Hein
and
Sabra Price

HEINEMANN
Portsmouth, NH

Heinemann
A division of Reed Elsevier Inc.
361 Hanover Street
Portsmouth, NH 03801-3912
Offices and agents throughout the world.

The authors and publisher wish to thank those who have generously given permission to reprint borrowed material.

Select samples of assessments developed and field-tested by the National Science Resources Center for the NSRC's Science and Technology for Children units of hands-on science instruction for elementary schools are reprinted here with permission of the NSRC. The NSRC is operated jointly by the Smithsonian Institution and the National Academy of Sciences. For information about the STC project, contact: NSRC, STC Project Director, Arts and Industries Building, Room 1201, Smithsonian Institution, Washington, D.C. 20560.

Library of Congress Cataloging-in-Publication Data

Hein, George E.
    Active assessment for active science : a guide for elementary
school teachers / by George E. Hein and Sabra Price.
        p.   cm.
    Includes bibliographical references.
    ISBN 0-435-08361-9 (acid-free paper)
    1. Science (Elementary)--Ability testing.   2. Science
(Elementary)--Examinations.   I. Price, Sabra.   II. Title.
    LB1585.H45   1994
    372.3'5--dc20
                                                            94-20529
                                                            CIP

Editor: Toby Gordon
Production: Melissa L. Inglis
Cover design: Darci Mehall
Cover illustration: Amanda McMonagle

Printed in the United States of America on acid-free paper.
09   08   07   06   EB   12   13   14   15

To
Seth, Rachel,
Willow, Jeffrey, Shawna,
Vinca, and Cora

Contents

Foreword
by Eleanor Duckworth   ix

Preface   xi

ONE
The Case for Active Assessment   1

TWO
Forms of Assessment   13

THREE
Managing Assessments   53

FOUR
Curriculum Developers Talk About Assessment   71

FIVE
Interpreting Children's Work   87

SIX
Scoring   111

SEVEN
Assessment and Educational Values   131

Works Cited   141

Selected Bibliography   143

Index   147

Foreword

Eleanor Duckworth
Harvard University

It is true this book is about assessment. It is also about many other things. It gives the reader a sense of the important dimensions of elementary science curriculum; of how to think about children's learning; of the many facets of a teacher's work; and of the relationships between teachers and parents, between individual classrooms and administrative systems, and between schools and communities. *Active Assessment for Active Science* raises questions about what education is all about.

It does this by looking honestly and broadly at the many ways that children can let us know what they are learning. Here are children seriously engaged in trying to understand how the material world functions in all of its diversity. How can a teacher appreciate their efforts and accomplishments, in order to decide how to take their learning further? "In other aspects of life…we draw on all the resources we can find to make an assessment," the authors point out (p. 13). Convincingly, they make the case that teachers can do the same.

The book includes some compelling discussions of the limits of multiple-choice tests. It seriously challenges the argument that test scores are more precise than any other form of information about children's learning. The authors make it clear that a number—say, 84—covers up what might be interesting about a child's work. How would anyone know whether that number represents a beautiful well-observed drawing, an ingenious invention of a way to compare how two high objects float, or an understanding of how the swing of a pendulum is affected when you stick some cotton batting onto the bob? Or how would anyone know whether that number indicates whether the child kept forgetting to water his plant or was fearful to make a prediction unless someone else had made one first? At the same time, Hein and Price point out that active assessments can lead to scoring systems which, while still being able to refer back to what children actually accomplished, can serve administrative needs.

The authors also underline the fact that language cannot be substituted for knowledge, understanding, care, confidence, or know-how. Encouraging children's own ways of expressing their thoughts allows a teacher to assess what they really understand far more easily than stressing the use of scientific terms. A phrase like *air pressure* is sometimes called upon to explain any phenomenon from the flight pattern of a butterfly to a surprising response of a balance beam—and deprives a teacher of any idea of how much the child actually understands. Knowing the technical terms like *suspension, solution, emulsion,* and *mixture* is no substitute for knowing the different ways that liquids and particles look, feel, and act when combined together. Children with limited knowledge of English can show that knowledge through their drawings or through the ways they interact with materials.

The greatest strength of this book, however, is that it makes clear just how intertwined assessment and teaching are. A teacher can barely do one without doing the other. And similarly, a teacher can barely report an appropriately active assessment without educating the parent, administrator, school committee, or community about the nature of elementary school science teaching. *Active Assessment for Active Science* calls for a great deal of such education. At the same time, it takes significant steps in showing us the way.

Preface

◆

In our work with almost a hundred school districts around the United States that are engaged in science education reform, we have been struck by how little is being done with assessments. Most districts report that they are buying more science materials for classrooms and developing systems to store and distribute them, designing appropriate inservice experiences for teachers, and connecting with outside agencies that want to support hands-on science education in the schools. But when it comes to assessing student learning, they report that they have not made comparable progress.

School administrators can act at the district level to bring in materials and provide professional development opportunities for teachers. In some cases they can even transfer textbook funds to buy materials. But changing assessment is more difficult. The traditions of testing are rooted deep in the educational system. One problem is the need to coordinate local, state, and national assessment activities; school systems are often reluctant to recommend active assessments if they are incompatible with state testing. At this time many states are reexamining their own assessment practices, and individual school systems are waiting for guidance from above.

In addition, school systems and individual teachers have many questions about active science assessments. What are they? What methods work? How are they connected? Can they be scored? What evidence of student learning can be translated into the summaries needed for districtwide use? We hope this book answers many of these questions.

Although the political issues involved in developing state and national assessment systems are beyond the scope of our discussion, we have articulated some of the problems of standardized testing and the advantages of active assessment and hope we can influence policy makers to increase their use of active assessments.

On a local level, we are convinced that active assessments can work. We have seen both individual classroom teachers and whole schools change their practice dramatically, producing records that enable educators

◆

to understand student learning and track children's progress for reasons of accountability. Above all, we hope this book will encourage classroom teachers to expand their efforts to document children's learning.

The assessments we discuss in this book have been described using a variety of terms, including *alternative, authentic, new, portfolio,* and *performance.* We feel none of these is adequate. Alternative assessment implies that our methods are a substitute for the real thing, which is hardly what we have in mind! We certainly believe that the approach we advocate is authentic, but so is standardized, multiple-choice testing, which can be an authentic measure of specific, albeit limited, skills. Active assessments are not new; they have a long history both within and outside formal education. And the use of any particular form of assessment, such as portfolio or performance, does not adequately cover the wide range of activities that can be used for assessment.

Active assessment provides a convenient label for a whole family of methods and simultaneously includes a nice reference to John Dewey. He used the word repeatedly to refer to learning that engaged the child, as distinct from "dead, useless" knowledge that was learned by rote. Dewey was concerned with relating school to life, with having children actively engaged in their own education, and in making schooling practical—all ideas that we associate with active assessments.

Dewey also distinguished between mere activity and the *meanings* that can be attributed to action. The active assessments we describe in this book are important and useful because we can interpret them; we can make meaning out of them. Children's drawings, writings, and performances are delightful activities in themselves, but they become powerful tools for assessment through methodical use. Just as hands-on science is only educationally valuable when it is used in the service of minds-on science, the products of that activity are particularly useful for assessment when we apply interpretive frameworks to them.

Dewey recognized that learning is an active process. He saw learning as the active engagement of the learner with her surroundings, not the process of an individual mind absorbing knowledge that exists independently. *Activity* was the word he used to reject this dualistic idea of the separation of the subject and object of learning.

Finally, Dewey stressed the social component of education, that school provides a model for the social interactions we should encourage to build a democratic society. Many active assessments capitalize on this idea, emphasizing group work, cooperative learning, and the connection of individual facts and ideas to the larger common knowledge base of the classroom community.

Just as in Dewey's time, these ideas are controversial. The constant stress on individual competition, on winners and losers, that is encouraged by standardized testing has served a purpose in our schools. It has led to labeling children as deficient, to tracking, and to a host of other subtle and not-so-subtle distinctions, many of which have been discriminatory to African Americans, girls, and other groups. Every major legal challenge about equity in schools has referred to the way test scores are used to sort children as evidence of discrimination. When we encourage assessment methods that stress what children know instead of what they don't know, that allow students to work cooperatively, and that acknowledge the diverse skills children bring to school regardless of their background, we are implicitly supporting the education of *all* children and making our schools more democratic and more inclusive. If this book contributes to these efforts we will be very pleased.

This book provides examples and ideas; it is not a *system* for assessment. Each teacher must develop her or his own combination of active assessments that fits with the teaching style, curriculum, and school climate. Active participation by each teacher in developing an appropriate system is as important as the active participation of children in their own learning. Democratic schooling requires that we provide for the active contributions of participants at every level. Teachers should have both the opportunity and the responsibility to influence the ways in which children are assessed.

The text that follows owes much to the help and support we have received from many people. Teachers all across the country who have been involved in the trial teaching of Science and Technology for Children units have generously provided their time and many of the examples included in this book. Curriculum developers Wendy Binder, Kathy Daiker, Patricia McGlashen, and David Hartney talked with us for hours to provide the material for Chapter 4. Our discussion of the interpretation of children's work owes much to our conversations with Brenda Engel, Anna Browder, Mimi Gurry, Kathy Stiles and Rhoda Kanevsky. Our ideas concerning classroom management were enriched by input from JoAnn DeMaria and Patricia McGlashen. Maryellen Harmon's work on equity in assessment contributed to the ideas found in Chapter 6. We benefited from our association with teachers in Lebanon, New Hampshire, as they developed active assessment for their district, as well as with Craig Altabell, Sally Laughlin, teachers in Cambridge, Massachusetts, and Kass Hogan from the Institute of Ecosystem Studies. For George, conversations about assessment during the biweekly meetings of the Videocase Studies in Science Project at TERC have been a constant reminder of the complex world that teachers inhabit. The opportunity to discuss our ideas at several meetings of the

North Dakota Study Group on Evaluation was invaluable in confirming that this approach was both legitimate and practical. Finally, there are those—Joyce Dutcher and Darlene Johnson, among others—who have generously shared material with us that it does not appear in the book, but has widened our knowledge of what is possible in the classroom. Although this list is long, it may be incomplete. We apologize to anyone we have omitted; it is inadvertent. We know that our ideas are inextricably embedded in the warm and supportive relationships we have with our colleagues.

ONE

The Case for Active Assessment

Assessment is integral to education; all teachers are concerned with what their students are learning and must devise systems for keeping track of students' progress. Teachers cannot answer the question, "What did I accomplish today?" merely by recalling what they've done—so much material covered, this classroom exercise carried out, those experiments completed by the students. They must also reflect on the possible outcomes for the students. Did they understand the material? What did they learn?

In this book we use the term *assessment* to encompass all the possible means whereby teachers make judgments about what students have learned. Tests—instruments specifically designed to measure student learning—are a subcategory of assessment. In the world of education, the word *test* has come to mean a paper-and-pencil exercise that is usually carried out silently and individually. The meaning of the word is, of course, broader. In the larger world, we speak of test pilots, drivers' tests, and tests of strength; any challenge can be a test. But the word is most likely to evoke images of sitting quietly at a desk, examination paper in front of us, filling in little circles, writing essays, or solving problems.

Tests are a tried and proven method for assessing learning. They have been used by teachers and government agencies for hundreds of years, and they provide a simple, direct, and impersonal way to find out something about a student. Because tests are so familiar and ubiquitous, in this first chapter we'll discuss why we're not satisfied with current science tests and talk about opportunities to widen the means of assessment by building on what we know from other fields. In the remainder of the book, we'll discuss the various forms of assessment available to teachers and ways to use them most effectively.

Why New Assessments?

Science education is being emphasized

The most obvious reason we need to consider new assessments in science is that science is increasingly important in the school curriculum. Newspapers, magazines, and professional literature feature articles about the central role of science in our lives, the significance of having a scientifically literate society, and the value of an education that includes science instruction. Although these articles have appeared for decades, the need for more science education is being stated more strongly and more frequently in today's increasingly technological world.

After the launch of the Russian spacecraft Sputnik in 1957, a wave of science education reforms, new science education materials, and support for science education swept the country. As a nation we felt the need to catch up with the Soviet Union. In the intervening years, other reasons have been advanced for improving science education: we need to be more environmentally aware, we need better thinking skills, we need to be able to participate more knowledgeably in the sociopolitical issues surrounding science-related topics. The most recent reason put forward is that the United States must remain competitive in the world economy.

Whatever the specific impetus, the pressure for more science in schools has steadily increased and has been backed by action. In the mid-1980s, the nation began spending millions of tax dollars to improve science education. The National Science Foundation, the major source of funding for science activities in this country, has an *increased* budget for science education at the same time its budget for science research has been *decreased*. Tens of millions of dollars have been spent on a series of new science curriculum projects: comprehensive (K–6) elementary school curriculums such as Education Development Center's (EDC) Insights, National Science Resources Center's (NSRC) Science and Technology for Children (STC), and the Full Option Science System (FOSS) developed at the University of California's Lawrence Hall of Science, as well as more targeted curriculums such as National Geographic's Kids Network, a computer-based science curriculum for upper elementary grades. Additionally, the competitive Statewide Systemic Initiative (SSI) program has so far committed two hundred and fifty million dollars over the next several years for statewide programs to improve science, mathematics, and technology education in twenty-five states. Additional SSI programs may be funded in future years. Another fifty-five million dollars a year is earmarked to increase the participation of underrepresented minorities in mathematics and science education. Funds are also designated for preservice and inservice teacher education. In addition to these tax dollars, private funds (as well as an enormous amount of time and effort) are provided by foundations, businesses, science museums, and other organizations.

The National Governors' Association's *National Education Goals* (1991), published as a result of the Bush-sponsored Governors' Conference on Education and endorsed by the Clinton administration, identifies six primary goals, all of them worthy. They include school readiness; high school completion; increased student achievement in all subjects and in citizenship; adult literacy and lifelong learning; safe, disciplined, drug-free schools; and the only curriculum-specific goal, to make the United States "lead the world" in mathematics and science achievement by the year 2000. It is therefore no surprise that every national organization involved in science education has issued proposals for new curriculums, science frameworks, or approaches to science education.

At the same time, a majority of states (either through their participation in the SSI program or independently) have initiated science education reforms. State frameworks have been drafted and statewide goals or targets are being set.

Professional science organizations, traditionally concerned primarily with research issues, higher education, and professional training, are also becoming involved in K–12 science education: committees have been formed, volunteers visit local schools, the subject is on the agenda at busy national meetings, and science education initiatives are being funded.

The current national effort to reform science education and increase its visibility and its significance in the school curriculum is unprecedented. It is more comprehensive than the effort made thirty-five years ago, has more political support from a larger constituency, and plays a more important role relative to the traditional science education profession. With science a more important part of the curriculum, the amount of time spent finding out what children have or have not learned in science inevitably increases and science assessment must be more comprehensive.

Accountability is increasing

This increased emphasis on science teaching coincides with an increased call for accountability in schools in general. Teachers are aware that more people are looking over their shoulders today than a decade ago, more forms need to be filled out, more questions are being asked by administrators, parents, and state auditors. Increased accountability inevitably brings with it more testing and other forms of assessment.

A *Nation at Risk* (National Commission on Excellence in Education 1983) paints a grim picture of schools and education and has received wide attention. One consequence is that schools are monitored more closely—specifically with regard to assessing student outcomes. Most of that assessment effort has been channeled into the narrow field of testing. At the national level, there is a movement to institute national assessments in science. The National Assessment of Educational Progress (NAEP), which gives tests in science to selected students every four years, now administers its tests to a much larger number of students, the intention being to generate data for state-by-state comparisons. A significant number of states mandate that every child at selected grade levels be tested, and almost all these tests include science assessments.

School budgets are decreasing

Despite the increased federal support for science education, many states and communities, facing budget crises as a result of decreasing voter support, are looking closely at what they spend for schools. As budgets shrink, school boards, city councils, and state legislatures suggest that less be spent for education. What is worth the money? What should be cut? Each component of the school budget requires supporting evidence. Science programs are especially vulnerable, since they require expenditures that stand out. Science specialists, science materials, and science field trips are easy targets in a time of retrenchment. Administrators need to generate evidence to support the value of their science programs, and assessment instruments can provide the means to do so.

Current tests are inadequate

Another reason we need to expand our approach to assessment and look at alternatives to traditional tests is our growing realization that these tests don't tell us what we want and need to know. The argument is twofold.

First, on the whole, the available tests are not very good: they are often poorly constructed, even when judged against their own criteria. They are not highly regarded by professionals in the science community, the education community, or even the psychometric community.

Second, even if the tests were all well constructed and were always carefully administered and thoughtfully scored, they would still be *inadequate*. Their format, requiring students to choose one of a few given answers or to fill in a blank, measures only a fraction of what we need to know about science learning.

Most science assessment in the United States is achieved through the tests contained in textbooks used by classroom teachers and through one of five major standardized commercial tests favored by school districts and state departments of education. The only comprehensive analysis of all the available tests used in elementary education was carried out almost twenty years ago by the Center for Studies in Evaluation (CSE) at UCLA (Hoepfner et al. 1976). The results were not encouraging. CSE developed criteria under four major headings—measurement validity, examinee appropriateness, administrative usability, and normed technical excellence—and ranked each test as excellent, fair, or poor in each of these categories. Of the fifty-eight science tests examined, none received a ranking of excellent in all four categories, and only three were ranked fair in all four! The rest were rated poor in at least one, if not more, of the four possible categories.

A much more recent study, *The Influence of Testing on Teaching Math and Science in Grades* 4–12 (Madaus et al. 1992), by the Center for the Study of Testing, Evaluation, and Educational Policy at Boston College comes to a similar conclusion. This study, described by its authors as the first "comprehensive nationwide study to examine commonly used tests, their influence on instruction, and the implications for the improvement of math and science instruction" (p. 3), concludes that today's tests "fall far short of the current standards recommended by math and science curriculum experts. . . . The tests most commonly taken by students—both standardized tests and textbook tests—emphasize and mutually reinforce low-level thinking and knowledge, and were found to have an extensive and pervasive influence on math and science instruction nationwide" (p. 1). The Boston College study focuses on the relationship between test item content and science topics, not on the technical quality of the tests. Nevertheless, the authors report that "approximately 20% of the items in standardized science tests, and 13% of those on textbook tests, contained ambiguities, potential for misconceptions, or used ethnic, gender, or culture stereotypic language" (p. 12).

Another way to judge the quality of traditional tests is to ask what they tell us about what children know or don't know. We frequently ask teachers to discuss test items. They are usually baffled that anyone could make decisions about student achievement on the basis of the results. They are shocked both by the small number of items on any topic and by the content of the questions. For example, one popular commercial test uses just four questions to determine what middle school students know about matter and energy. One question asks the student to select the correct meaning of a technological word from among four choices, a second question asks whether measuring three linear dimensions provides information about an object's density, weight, mass, or volume, and the remaining two questions—on electricity and mechanics—ask for answers based on drawings that are, to us, ambiguous. Tests like these do not adequately assess science learning.

Science curriculums have changed

Another reason we need to rethink science assessment is that the content of science curriculums has changed. We've already discussed the tremendous growth in science education in the past decade. Not just *more* science, but *different* science is being taught. The new curriculums are qualitatively different in form and content from previous commercial textbooks. The emphasis now is on a combination of "hands-on" and "minds-on" science. Many new projects stress the active participation of children in *doing* science rather than learning *about* science, learning the content of science while engaging in its processes.

In addition, the motives for teaching science have expanded. Besides learning content, students are expected to think scientifically, to act like scientists, and to feel positive about science. Tests simply aren't sufficient to assess all the components of a modern, comprehensive science education program; a broader approach is needed. (Figure 1–1 relates the purposes of science education to the capabilities of traditional tests.)

One objective of most science programs is that children learn some facts and concepts about science. It is feasible to assess such learning through multiple-choice tests, although assessing conceptual knowledge in this way is more difficult than assessing factual knowledge. That may be why the Boston College study found that among the most widely used science tests "three fourths of the items on standardized tests and 90% of those on textbook tests sampled recall and routine application thinking" (Madaus, p. 12).

Science education could focus on one or more of the following:	Possibility of assessment with multiple-choice, paper-and-pencil tests:
Facts	Feasible
Concepts	Feasible, but difficult

Skills/processes
    General: "scientific method"
    Specific: measure, observe, etc.
	Very difficult or impossible

Attitudes	Almost impossible
Being a scientist, doing science	Impossible

Figure1-1 *The capabilities of traditional tests to assess possible components of science education.*

But there are additional reasons for teaching science. Students should learn two kinds of skills and processes. One is higher-order thinking skills, sometimes referred to as "the scientific method," which include such mental processes as interpreting data, drawing conclusions, and hypothesizing. The other is actual physical skills—observing, measuring, and using scientific instruments. It is conceivable that the thinking skills could be assessed through standardized tests, although this is quite difficult and, in practice, rarely happens. The Boston College study found that 92% of the standardized test items and 95% of textbook tests did not refer to processes or skills of any kind.

The second category of skills, actually doing something, cannot be measured by a pencil-and-paper test at all. You can't tell whether anyone can manipulate anything in the real world—play a musical instrument, drive a car, swim (three physical skills routinely assessed through performance assessment)—without having the person carry out the activity. Similarly, in science, you can't tell whether someone can use a ruler, a microscope, or a spectrograph unless the person demonstrates that skill.

Finally, besides wanting our children to *do* science, we are interested in children's attitudes toward science. Although paper-and-pencil tests give us some information about what people report about themselves, this is only a superficial reflection of their attitudes in practice. It is almost impossible to determine to what extent someone actually enjoys doing science without extending our assessments beyond paper-and-pencil testing.

New ideas about learning have surfaced

The final reason we need to rethink assessment comes from current views about how students learn and how they express their learning. In order for students to learn, they need to be actively engaged, to explore and initiate action, so they can derive meaning from what they do. In addition, educators now value group activity, discussion, and reflection as ways to facilitate learning. The new catchwords for these ideas, *constructivism* and *cooperative learning*, describe concepts that go back almost a century. Individually administered tests that only require students to respond to problems and questions determined by the examiner and that limit responses to filling small circles or writing in the letter designating the chosen response do not assess learning as defined by constructivism and collaborative learning.

Assessment ideas appropriate for these learning concepts also have new descriptors. *Authentic assessment, active assessment, performance assessment,* and *portfolio assessment* all refer to approaches that are consonant with active learning styles. The growing interest in these new forms of assessment is a clear signal that we need to change the way we assess students, that we need to move beyond traditional testing. And the resources for developing newer, active assessments for science education are at hand.

The Opportunity for Active Assessment

National and state trends

Support for new forms of assessment comes from national, state, and local activities. We indicated earlier that the current emphasis on science education is different not only in degree but also in kind from previous science education. This qualitative difference applies to assessment as well. For example, the expanded NAEP is also changing the way science is assessed. In 1994 NAEP, for the first time, included performance tasks, open-ended items, and collected student work over time (such as portfolios) as part of the assessment. The *Science Framework* for the 1994 assessment, in a break with tradition, stipulated that multiple-choice items should take no more than 50% of students' time.

Several national groups have recently advocated national testing. One of these, the influential National Standards Committee, envisions a national examination system very different from the kinds of tests we are accustomed to. They propose an examination *system*, a collection of examinations, performance assessments, portfolios, and examples of student work. The National Committee on Science Education Standards and Assessment, established under the auspices of the National Academy of Science, has begun to develop science standards for the United States. In 1992, the Academy set up three working committees on curriculum, instruction, and assessment, but the assessment group felt that it could not do its work independently of the other two committees and has stressed that assessment needs to take into account the "full range of goals of science education, not simply those that have traditionally been measured" (National Committee on Educational Standards and Assessment 1993, p. 12).

Finally, as states have begun to expand and reform science education, a significant number are also developing alternative assessments. In Massachusetts, for example, the state assessment program, MAEP, has included open-ended questions in reading, mathematics, and science since 1988, adding practical, problem-solving tasks in mathematics and science in 1989 (Badger and Thomas 1989; Badger, Thomas, and McCormack 1990). The New York State Department of Education (n.d.) began to administer practical tasks to *every* fourth-grade student in 1989. Students circulate among five stations set up in the classroom and use a balance, a thermometer, and a ruler; sort objects; and test an electric circuit. The Department of Education staff believes that this performance test provides significant information about the level of science education in all schools in the state and, by example, promotes an increase in hands-on science instruction. In addition, since this test is administered to 200,000 children annually, it demonstrates that large-scale performance testing is feasible. A number of other states, including California, Connecticut, and Minnesota, have begun to develop elaborate science assessment systems that involve performance tasks for students, open-ended questions, and the assessment of students' work over time.

Changes in language arts assessment

The backbone of U.S. education is the teaching of reading and the other language arts. More instructional time is spent teaching this subject than any other; in some classrooms language arts instruction may take the majority of the school day. In the past decade, the teaching of reading has changed dramatically as an increasing number of schools have shifted to some form of whole language teaching, embracing the view that learning to read is primarily a matter of students' making sense out of text rather than learning how to decode a symbol system and that all aspects of language acquisition need to be addressed. This change in the fundamental conception of the act of reading has brought with it an equally fundamental change in assessment. It was the reading community that introduced the idea of authentic assessment in general and portfolio assessment specifically.

The basic argument for changing assessment in whole language instruction is that in order to understand what a child knows, that child needs to perform the essential act of reading, that is, draw meaning out of text. Since it is possible for a reader to derive meaning from text even if she makes technical mistakes in decoding (misperceiving a word or tense, for example), the degree of mastery of reading cannot be determined by counting up errors in grammar, word meaning, or pronunciation; it requires a more comprehensive analysis of the student's performance. In addition, a range of other activities associated with reading—writing, distinguishing various approaches to reading, understanding the concept of what it means to read—needs to be considered in assessing whole language acquisition. Thus, whole language instruction advocates that children be given the opportunity to use language in authentic, rich, and varied ways and that assessment be carried out in like manner. It stresses conducting ongoing evaluation, using behavior as an indicator of underlying competence, and employing informal as well as formal means, and it rejects most traditional, multiple-choice reading tests.

The assessments that we advocate for science education are similar to those in whole language programs: they use various means to find out what meaning children make of the natural world and how they express that meaning. These active assessments are congruent with instructional activities. They allow teachers to base their instruction on the information the assessments provide about children's progress.

New curriculum projects

Developing new forms of assessment was an important element of many of the new curriculum projects, and a number of them include explicit and varied ways to find out what students learn. (Some curriculum developers discuss their approach to assessment in Chapter 4.)

Assessment activities for EDC's Insights curriculum include an introductory questionnaire that serves as a probe to find out what students understand before they begin; embedded assessments (activities during the course of the unit that can inform the teacher of students' progress); some extended problems; and a final assessment that includes both a written (not short-answer!) section and performance tasks. This collection of activities, along with daily assignments and children's directed and open-ended work, constitutes the assessment framework.

FOSS units include an assessment "package" that always involves hands-on assessment (students work with materials); pictorial assessment (students answer questions based on pictures of experimental setups and results of investigations); and, finally, a reflective assessment (students answer more traditional kinds of science questions).

NSRC's STC curriculum units contain a set of assessments designed to be used together in order to profile each student's learning. Many of these are woven into, or embedded, within the lessons, and they use a range of formats. They include students' work products, science notebooks, and drawings, as well as more formalized assessments, such as matched pre/postactivities.

These three new curriculum projects, although they vary somewhat in the details, all stress the need for multiple forms of assessment, integrated with teaching and designed so that assessment requires children to carry out activities similar to those recommended for instruction.

Research studies on children's understanding

Over the past twenty years, an increasing number of researchers all over the world have been exploring children's thinking in science, examining children's conceptions, asking what they understand and don't understand, and elucidating how they make sense out of the natural world—how their minds work as they interact with objects and forces in nature. Teachers address similar issues when they assess students in their classrooms.

One striking feature of the research on children's thinking is that it almost *never* uses multiple-choice questions or other short-answer forms. The research studies use in-depth interviews, children's drawings, thinking-aloud protocols (in which children are asked to solve some problem and talk about what they are doing while they do it), videotapes of children's activities, and other means that parallel those advocated by educational assessment reformers.

Researchers have also realized the enormous complexity of finding out how children think about science. The way children respond to some bit of the natural world depends a great deal on how they encounter it. Children react differently to a stranger's questions than to those that arise in their classroom peer groups. Children react differently in an environment rich with materials and the freedom to explore them than in a tightly controlled setting with few items to manipulate. A child's responses in a setting that allows repeated opportunities to discuss and interact may be quite different from a response solicited only once. Lillian McDermott, a physicist, argues that "because results and methods are so closely intertwined in research on conceptual understanding, it is important in interpreting findings to bear in mind the procedures used" (1984, p. 26). She lists the following characteristics that need to be considered in interpreting results and warns that these contextual parameters are never considered in traditional testing situations:

> Nature of the instrument used to assess understanding.
>
> Degree of interaction between student and investigator.
>
> Depth of probing.
>
> Form of data.
>
> Physical setting.
>
> Time frame.
>
> Goals of the investigator. (p. 26)

The importance of this range of factors adds weight to the argument that assessment should be embedded into instruction if it is going to give us a meaningful picture of what a child knows and understands.

Conclusion

It's time for new assessments in science education. To do science, children must interact with the physical world—drop objects, observe butterfly larvae, measure length and speed, plant seeds and watch the seedlings sprout, build electric circuits and test them—and they must participate in the world of ideas—design experiments, test theories, hypothesize, predict, discuss, and argue. The only way to assess the rich and varied experiences that constitute doing science is to devise ways for the actions and their products to become part of assessment. If the assessment of science is limited to passive responses, we will never fully understand what our students know. Assessing science through paper-and-pencil tests is akin to assessing a basketball player's skills by giving a written test. We may find out what someone knows *about* basketball, but we won't know how well that person plays the game.

Changing the way in which we assess science requires enormous effort. Teachers need to think differently about their classrooms and their materials, and about how they organize their time and how they interact with students. Principals need to rethink what they ask of teachers, administrators need to accept different kinds of evidence, and policy makers need to recognize the significance of new indicators. Parents have to be led to accept the different forms of reporting that the schools will be sending home. We must make this effort, and the rewards when we do will be great.

Forms of Assessment

· ◆ ·

Anything students do can be used for assessment purposes. If we limit our thinking about assessment to ideas derived from traditional testing, we often end up with paper-and-pencil exercises. If, however, we consider assessment as using our senses to find out what someone else is thinking, we more readily comprehend the diverse forms available to us. In other aspects of life, we use all available information to determine what our friends think, to judge what our children can accomplish, or to assess the qualifications of a carpenter, a plumbing-and-heating business, or a babysitter. It is considered reasonable to try to "read" a person's facial expressions, to question friends and neighbors, to review a sample of the person's (or organization's) work. In short, we draw on all the resources we can find to make an assessment.

A similar range of resources is available to an elementary school science teacher. It is possible to observe children, talk with them, photograph them, tape-record their conversations, and collect the products of their work, whether written, drawn, or in some other format. In this chapter we describe different forms of science assessments and provide examples from actual curriculums in real classrooms. The examples are intended to be just that—examples, not models. We have chosen them because each has been useful to teachers and school systems; they are not prescriptions for what should be done. Some new science curriculums provide teachers with a range of options for assessment. But creating the right instrument for a particular curriculum unit can also be an individual matter, reflecting what a teacher has actually done with the students, who the students are, how old they are, the amount of time that can be given to the assessment, and the purpose of the assessment. The assessment tools used in any classroom may also reflect a teacher's overall teaching experience as well as her experience teaching the particular science units that form the curriculum: an assessment appropriate the first time a unit is taught may not be

◆

necessary the third or fourth time she presents the same material. Similarly, although a teacher initially may not use some activities that can serve as assessments, he may incorporate them into his teaching after a year or two of experience.

While every assessment idea presented here comes from activities carried out by one or more teachers, no teacher does (or should try to do) all of them. They are presented as examples of actual practice, each of which may be useful to you but any of which may be unsuitable for a particular situation.

It is relatively easy to suggest time-consuming assessment and documentation schemes; it is much more difficult to carry them out within the time constraints of an ordinary classroom and in conjunction with all the other tasks demanding attention and all the other responsibilities that fall on your shoulders as a teacher. We have deliberately presented a wide range of assessments in the hope that some will fit your opportunities and constraints.

For our teaching to be effective we must provide students with opportunities to construct, apply, and restate concepts. Similarly, assessments should also provide different ways for children to express themselves and to apply and restate their understandings about the world.

Pre/Postunit Assessment Activities

A powerful idea in assessment, derived more from research and national assessments than from classroom practice, is the concept of pre/posttests. Lots of assessments don't require this complex arrangement: most often assessments are only used to determine what a child can do after instruction. After all, there isn't much need for a pretest when a teacher knows that the children have had no experience with what is going to be taught. A beginning foreign language class doesn't have to start with a pretest. But the influence of research designs on educational practice is strong, and pre- and posttests are now commonly used by classroom teachers, incorporated into curriculum materials, and referred to in year-to-year comparisons of national and state tests.

Many teachers use preinstruction activities to find out what children know before they are introduced to new material. Such introductory lessons take on real significance when teachers understand that children's own conceptions should be taken into account in teaching. But the activity that is most useful for finding out what is in (or on!) children's minds before starting a lesson may have to be modified somewhat in order to make it a useful pretest that can later be matched with the posttest.

The most powerful argument for matched pre/postunit assessments is that they can demonstrate that students know more about a subject at the end of the curriculum unit than at its beginning. Pre/post assessments can be traditional tests, but they need not be. The key is that the assessment activities are *identical* and therefore produce comparable results. However, it is also possible to compare two similar activities (written observations or lab write-ups, for example) early and late in teaching a science unit. If you are designing pre/postunit assessments, there are several things to bear in mind:

1. Decide what it is you expect students to learn and what you want to measure. This may be *content*, information about a subject; a *skill*, such as using a microscope, making accurate observations, recording, measuring, or setting up an experiment; or an *attitude*, such as sensitivity toward living things, appropriate feelings about death, or interest in science. To be a useful pre/postassessment, what you ask the students to do must allow them to demonstrate the outcome you want to assess.

2. Remember that there is no one correct format. Pre/postunit assessments can be drawings, conversations, journal entries, or experiments. They may assess group or individual knowledge. You should base the form of the assessment on what it is you want to find out and on the nature of the science activities in the unit. What matters is that you end up with two comparable sets of data that assess something of importance.

3. Make sure the two activities have the same form and structure if they are not identical. A postunit assessment that requires students to organize knowledge in a different way from the preunit assessment may be a perfectly legitimate and appropriate assessment task, but you may be unable to compare the two. If a pretest provides visual clues or defines technical vocabulary, these same clues and definitions should be provided on the posttest.

4. In assessing baseline knowledge through a preunit activity, a good rule to keep in mind is: if students don't know the material, don't ask them about it. Although it can be tempting to ask students something they know nothing about but should learn during the unit, this may make them feel inadequate or stupid, even though they would later shine on the postunit test. Try instead to find an activity your students will be able to complete despite their lack of knowledge about or their unfamiliarity with the specific content.

5. Do not present your preunit test as a test, and never grade it. The atmosphere should be one of discovering what students know to begin the instructional process, not judging the state of their knowledge.

Brainstorming

This activity may be familiar to your students, particularly in the primary grades, although most teachers use it only early in a unit. However, conversations related to the content of the curriculum can be carried out at the beginning *and* end of the unit. The prompts can be general ("What do you know about plants?") or more specific ("How would you test foods for fat? How could you tell time if you didn't have a clock?"). Finding a juicy, engaging question or situation that is likely to elicit curriculum-related discussions can be difficult and takes considerable thought. Specific, focused questions grounded in students' lives and experiences and at the same time closely related to activities central to the unit seem to work best. Asking first graders, "Can you describe the weather outside?" is more likely to elicit what they know about weather than asking them, "What do you know about the weather?"

Brainstorming for assessment and for instruction is not always the same. When the goal is to measure learning, the question or topic should be related to what students will be investigating so that you will later be able to use the discussion to document and assess growth in that area. When brainstorming serves as an introductory instructional activity, questions may be formulated to discover what students know in general, rather than what they know and don't know about some specific topic.

The STC curriculum provides two examples of brainstorming topics used pre- and postunit. In the sixth-grade unit *Ecosystems* students discuss how living things depend on one another, and in *Floating and Sinking* fourth graders are asked, "What do you think makes objects float or sink?"

To be sure you will have a preunit assessment for each student, ask everyone to take a moment to record (and date) their thoughts either in science notebooks or on separate sheets of paper before the whole-class conversation begins. (Some teachers ask students to decorate their science notebook covers with their ideas, making the activity less like a "test.") The exercise of writing before they talk will also lead to a more engaged class discussion, because the students will have focused on the topic and thought about what they want to say. Before you begin the group discussion at the end of the unit, again ask the students to record what they know individually. (See "What I Know About Chemicals" on page 92 for an example of a written pre/postunit assessment.)

Another widely used format is to ask students to record what they know and what they want to know about a topic at the beginning of the unit. Then, at the end, ask them to record what they found out. This format is often referred to as a KWL (Know, Want to know, and Learned) chart. "What do I know?" may be too general a question for some children, burdening them with the task of generating information about something even if they know nothing; the result may be random guesses and textbooklike answers that use words the children don't understand. It is worth the effort to come up with a specific and personally engaging question, because such questions help children draw on their own experience and bring forward the knowledge they have. Good questions allow for speculation and discourage closure, so there is no possibility that a quick student can end the conversation by providing the "answer."

Many curriculums combine brainstorming discussions used as pre- and postunit assessments with another activity—drawing or writing for example. In *Ecosystems* students look at a picture of a woodland scene and write about what would change if a pioneer family built a home there. The following pair of pre- and postunit writings indicates that the student has a more extensive understanding of ecology after the unit than before:

> If a pioneer family moved in the animals may get frightened and run away, it might not be very peaceful anymore. (10/20/92)

> If a pioneer family moved right in the middle of a forest I think lots of important things would happen like: they would have to cut down trees to make the house, when they build the house they might create land slids because [what] if the built the house by a river and create land slids by all the mud that goes into the river, also the house might start pollution if the have a chimney all the smoke goes into the air and create acid rain, and last but not least is that people would probably fish to get food so the population in the river might go down. (1/14/93)

If you aren't going to use the brainstorming list for individual student evaluations, post it in the classroom and revisit it occasionally with your students to record their evolving concepts. In some classrooms, students correct inaccuracies on the list and add new ideas, questions, and information.

First lab report or observation/last lab report or observation

Having students perform a task, such as observing and recording plant growth, conducting a lab test, or designing an experiment, early in a unit or semester and then asking them to repeat the task late in the unit or semester, may allow you to document skill development (formatting graphs and tables, planning experiments, and recording observations) as well as changes in attitudes.

Here is an early observation recorded in a fourth grader's science notebook:

> 9/18/90 When I looked through the microscope at an onion skin I thought it looked wet, kind of drops of water were on it. What I thought was water was actually [end of entry]

Two months later, the same fourth grader made this entry:

> 11/21/90 Yesterday we looked at sea monkeys and their eggs under a microscope. The eggs were big and brown and roundish. The sea monkeys were clear with a bright orange stripe down the middle. (It's funny because orange is such a bright color and you can't see it even with a hand lens.) They moved in spurts, as if they were jerking forward, stopping for a split second, and jerking forward again. The sea monkey had six little legs, or fins (I couldn't tell which) and I think they use them to swim about, but they probably use their tails too.

Clearly, this student's involvement and interest in science has increased, as has her ability or willingness to make detailed and speculative observations. (The entire journal is discussed in greater detail in Chapter 5.)

If students have been using prepared sheets and tables on which to record their observations and experiments, you might ask them to set up their own recording sheets at the end of the unit; knowing how to organize and communicate information is an important skill, and seeing how well they can do so on their own is a useful assessment. If you make the task more complex in this way, however, this particular activity can't legitimately serve as a matched pre/postassessment.

Content-specific tasks and demonstrations

You can design your own pre/postunit test for a particular curriculum by identifying what you want to assess and designing a simple way to measure that learning. Providing actual materials for students to observe or work with is helpful.

In the STC unit *Floating and Sinking*, for example, fourth graders write up explanations of what happens when their teacher places an acrylic bead in salt water and then in fresh water. This activity is repeated at the end of the unit and relates directly to several of the lessons. Figures 2–1a and 2–1b show one student's responses.

LESSON 1

Recording Sheet **Activity Sheet 1**

Name: ____________________

Date: 11-17-92

What did you see happening?

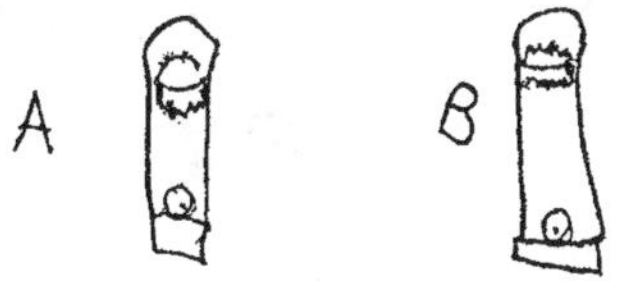

What are at least two reasons you can think of for what you observed?

1. Reason (B) I think the bead sunk slowly because it probaly cold.

2. Reason (A) I think the bead sunk fast because it was probaly warm.

3. Fish Float because their fins keep them up.

Figure 2-1a A *student's preunit assessment from the* STC Floating and Sinking *unit.*

Questionnaires

EDC's Insights curriculum project incorporates preunit questionnaires as one way to determine student knowledge, and in some units the same questionnaire, in whole or in part, is repeated at the end of the unit. In the second-grade unit *Growing Things*, the questionnaire can also be presented orally. It combines specific content-knowledge questions with ones that are more open-ended. Question 8, shown in Figure 2–2, is used on both the pre- and postquestionnaire.

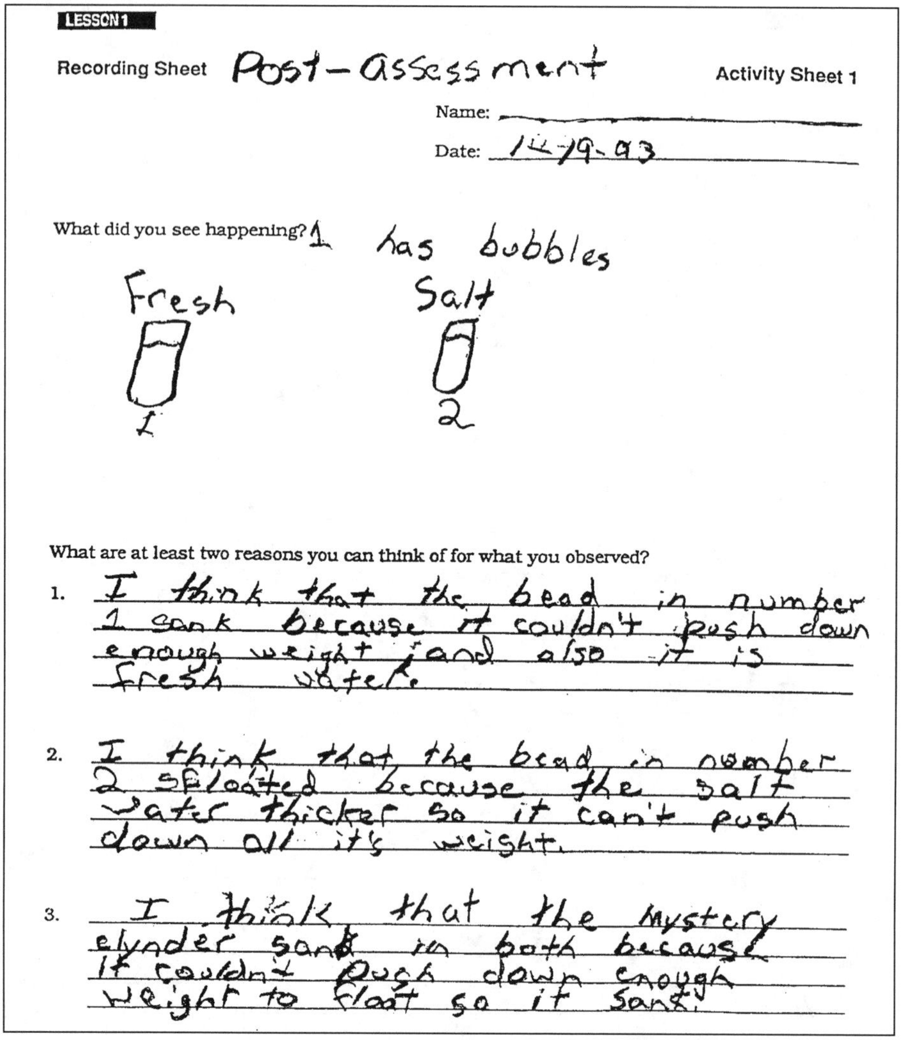

LESSON 1

Recording Sheet Post-assessment Activity Sheet 1

Name: ______

Date: 12-19-93

What did you see happening? 1 has bubbles

Fresh 1

Salt 2

What are at least two reasons you can think of for what you observed?

1. I think that the bead in number 1 sank because it couldn't push down enough weight and also it is fresh water.

2. I think that the bead in number 2 floated because the salt water thicker so it can't push down all it's weight.

3. I think that the mystery clynder sank in both because it couldn't push down enough weight to float so it sank.

Figure 2-1b *The same student's postunit assessment from the* STC Floating and Sinking *unit.*

Drawings

This is an excellent pre/postunit assessment format to use wherever you can appropriately fit it in. It is quick to administer, is simple and non-threatening, does not exclude students with reading or writing problems, and has the potential to document dramatic change. Drawings also offer students clear and direct feedback on their own learning. Teachers of young children report that pre/postunit drawings help their students see how much they have learned and that students are both impressed and excited by examining their own work.

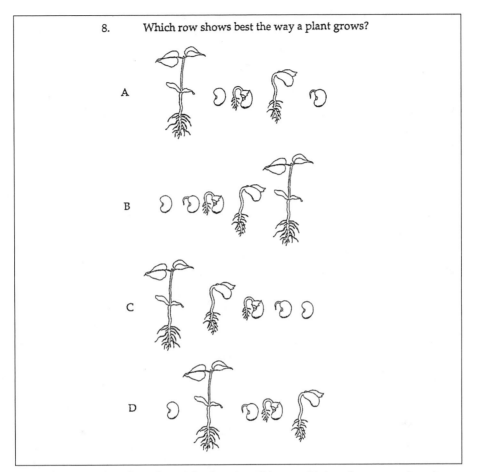

8. Which row shows best the way a plant grows?

Figure 2-2 A *question from the* Insights Growing Things *unit's introductory questionnaire, repeated postunit.*

Drawings are successfully incorporated in the STC *Butterflies* curriculum for second grade, in which students draw pictures of caterpillars and butterflies before and after the unit. In STC's *Electric Circuits*, for grades four and five, students draw pictures of light bulbs (dissected during the unit) before and after they carry out this activity.

In STC's first-grade curriculum *Organisms*, students begin by drawing a picture of something that is alive and those things that it needs to stay alive. This activity is repeated at the end of the unit. The drawings in Figures 2–3 and 2–4 exemplify the rich results that are possible. (The text in the drawings was dictated by the students.)

Figure 2-3a *A first grader's STC Organisms preunit drawing.*

Figure 2-3b *The same student's STC Organisms postunit drawing.*

Figure 2-4a *Another first grader's* STC Organisms *preunit drawing.*

Figure 2-4b *The same student's* STC Organisms *postunit drawing.*

Concept maps

A concept map, which is similar to a curriculum web, diagrams the relationships between different concepts. For example, a map starting out with the word *ocean* in the center would include as many related concepts as a student could think of: what the ocean is composed of, the living and nonliving things in the ocean and the relationships between them, how humans use the ocean, and so forth. Some people claim that misconceptions are revealed both through incorrect concept links and important links that are omitted.

While concept maps are usually used as a tool to encourage students to reflect on their learning (Novak and Gowin 1986), they can also be used for assessment. They can provide a picture of what each child thinks and knows about a topic before a science unit or course of study and at its end. Alternatively, a concept map can be drawn at the outset of a unit and new links can be added in other colors as the unit progresses, documenting a student's (or a class's) evolving thinking.

As with many of the other forms of assessment described in this book, students may need practice before they can use this tool fully and before their maps reliably represent their knowledge. Concept maps have been used with children of all ages, from first grade through high school.

Observation

Teacher observations are a primary source of information about student learning, and informal observations take place continuously. Most teachers develop a sense of who knows what and who is having trouble with which concepts through such observations. But like all forms of assessment, the key to converting informal observation into assessment is to decide what student actions and behaviors you will observe to assess progress. Here are some guidelines:

- Observing how students solve problems, troubleshoot malfunctioning equipment, or try to figure out why an experiment is unsuccessful indicates how they apply knowledge. (For example, during one physical science unit in which students were building equipment, the teacher overheard students discussing which part to wiggle, pull out, or straighten.)

- Noticing when and how students relate information from trade books to what they are doing in class can illuminate how they assimilate information. (In a second-grade class studying pollination, one student listened to a story describing bees and then used that information to correctly identify a dead bee she found on the playground.)

- Listening to conversations and discussions can provide evidence of the appropriate use of new vocabulary. (Similar evidence can come from labels on drawings and notebook entries.)

- Watching students perform a science skill reveals how well they do it and their understanding of the concepts behind it. (For example, do they begin a linear measurement at zero? Do they double-check their measurements or assume that their first measurements are correct? In using a microscope, are they tilting the mirror the wrong way to catch the light? Are they focusing on the dust on the slide instead of the object?)

Classroom teachers have a large number of students to observe, and a science unit usually has many learning goals. Therefore, every teacher needs some systematic way to keep track of observations. Without a system, it is too easy to forget to observe important activities, too easy to overlook some students. Although you will of course need to figure out your own system, the methods described in Chapter 3 will start you off.

Prediction Activities

Prediction is central to scientific study and research. It requires that you use the knowledge you have at a given time to foretell what will happen under a given set of circumstances. Unlike guesses, predictions are based on knowledge and can therefore be used to assess thinking and learning. You can build both formal and informal prediction activities into your curriculum for this purpose.

Discussions

You can incorporate the making of predictions into discussions either with an individual student or with groups of students. Let's look at two situations in which students in a second-grade classroom studying butterflies were asked to make predictions that revealed their knowledge about metamorphosis. In the first, the teacher read a book to his class about a caterpillar; partway through he asked his students to predict what would happen to it. In the second, toward the end of the unit when most of the chrysalises had opened and butterflies emerged, the teacher asked his class to predict what they thought would happen to the few remaining unopened ones. His students responded with a range of answers that revealed their ideas about death and the changes that might result in the emergence, or nonemergence, of butterflies. This sort of class discussion is commonplace, but not all teachers realize that such exchanges contain assessment data that can be systematically recorded and used, and that these prediction-type conversations can be planned.

Prediction activity sheets

It is possible to design "prediction sheets" on which students make predictions about given situations. A series of such sheets spaced throughout a science unit has the potential to document a student's increasing understanding of the material. Certain science topics lend themselves more easily to this format than do others. They fit naturally into STC's unit on electricity, for example. The sheets in Figures 2–5a, b, and c are from *Electric Circuits*.

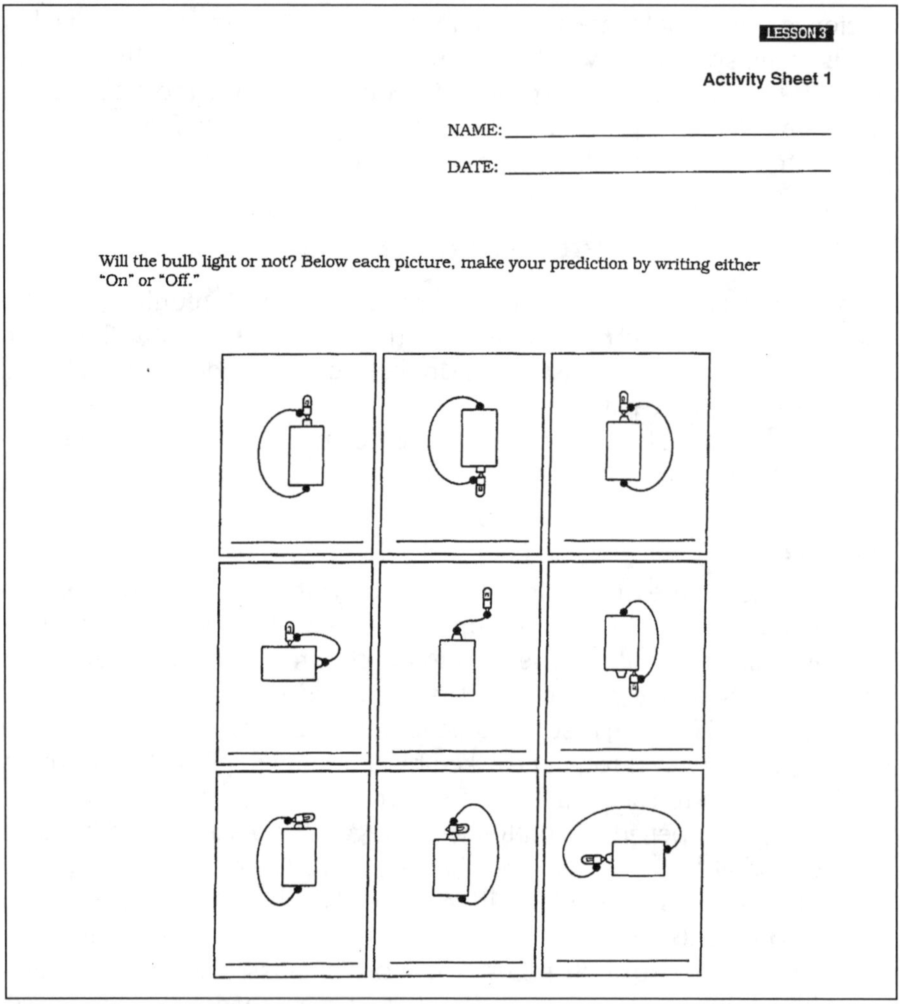
LESSON 3

Activity Sheet 1

NAME: ______________________

DATE: ______________________

Will the bulb light or not? Below each picture, make your prediction by writing either "On" or "Off."

Figure 2-5a *A prediction activity sheet from Lesson 3 in* STC's Electric Circuits *unit.**

*From the National Science Resources Center's Science and Technology for Children unit entitled *Electric Circuits*, ©1991, National Academy of Sciences, Washington, D.C.

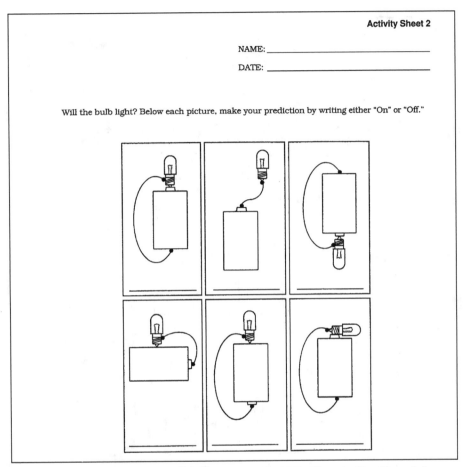

Activity Sheet 2

NAME: _____

DATE: _____

Will the bulb light? Below each picture, make your prediction by writing either "On" or "Off."

Figure 2-5b *A prediction activity sheet from Lesson 6 in STC's Electric Circuits unit.* *

Data recording sheets

Ongoing data collection sheets can provide a running record of predictions over time. Students can be asked to collect experimental data over a number of days, using each day's data to predict their next findings. Second graders studying STC's *Plant Growth and Development* recorded the growth of FastPlants® (*Brassica rapa*) over a period of days; each day they predicted the growth they expected to measure the following day. An examination of the data sheets demonstrated that some students' predictions were based on the data they had recorded. The table on page 29 is representative.

*From the National Science Resources Center's Science and Technology for Children unit entitled *Electric Circuits*, ©1991, National Academy of Sciences, Washington, D.C.

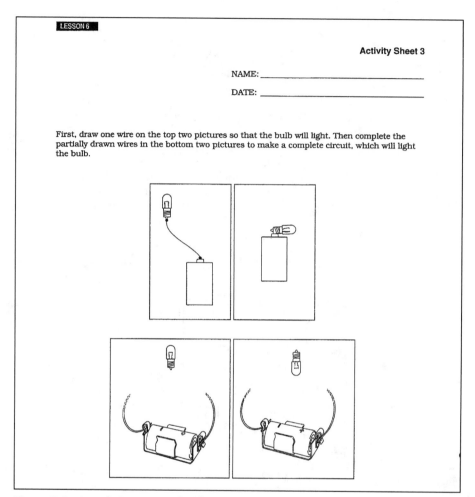

Figure 2-5c *A prediction activity sheet from Lesson 6 in STC's Electric Circuits unit.**

Looking at this table, we can surmise that this student probably scaled down her predictions from six to four and from six to five in response to the actual measurements. We can confirm this by talking with her about it.

Written predictions

Asking students to write out their predictions during the course of a unit can also serve as an embedded assessment. In STC's *Ecosystems* unit,

---

*From the National Science Resources Center's Science and Technology for Children unit entitled *Electric Circuits*, ©1991, National Academy of Sciences, Washington, D.C.

Height today	Height Prediction
3 cm	6 cm
3 1/2	4
4 1/2	6
4 1/2	5
5	8
6	8

students build and observe an aquarium (and later a terrarium). They are asked to predict what would happen if all of the plants in the aquarium died. One student responded:

> If this aquarium had no plants the animals would die because of no air and the aquarium would be rell dirty because the smails also be dirty. Even if the fish lived they would have no food and no place to shelter therslefs. That paraghrafh is another good reason to have plants.

Embedded Products and Activities

Embedded assessments occur in the context of the unit and within the flow of the lessons. They might be activities that naturally occur in a lesson but are used as assessment, or something extra that students are asked to do but that follows naturally from what they are already doing. From the students' point of view, embedded assessments look like part of the unit even if the activity has been designated by a curriculum developer or teacher as an assessment exercise.

Products as embedded assessments

In some science units, the students' products provide evidence of whether or not they followed directions, were successful at troubleshooting, or applied previously learned knowledge. Here are some examples of program products:

- In units on plants, students may grow plants and/or make flower models. The plants grown by students indicate that they planted the seeds and watered and cared for the plants. The appearance of seeds in units based on FastPlants® indicate the plants have been successfully pollinated. A flower model indicates how well a student understands a flower's component parts.

- In units on electricity, students are often asked to construct complete electric circuits (parallel and series, for example) and then, after learning how to make a switch, to design and build a flashlight. In the later stages of units they may build a working electromagnet, followed by a motor, or they may wire a doll house. In order to successfully complete any of these tasks, students have to apply everything previously learned.

- When students use microscopes, their drawings of what they observe often indicate whether they know what they're doing or are just going through the motions. For example, drawings can provide powerful proof that students have successfully found a range of living objects in a drop of pond water. Drawings copied from an illustration will be equally obvious.

- In many science units students are asked to identify the variables in a situation and design an experiment. Their experimental plan is a product you can evaluate to discover whether they know how to set up a fair test. In some units students carry out this activity individually and in others it is a team effort. In the STC *Ecosystem* unit, for example, students must individually design an experiment to find out if an ice cube with salt on it melts faster or slower than an ice cube with no salt on it. In this case, you would look for evidence of:
  - A systematic approach.
  - The use of controls, such as starting at the same time or setting up the ice cubes in the same location.
  - An attempt to record the ice cubes' sizes.
  - Record keeping.

Students can also be asked to use the products they make. For example, in a weather unit, students might first make and then use compasses, wind indicators, and anemometers. In a study of magnets and motors, students could be asked to make a compass spin using magnets and electrical current. In a unit on time students might make and then use different timing devices. How students use their products often shows how well they understand their function.

Lessons as embedded assessments

An entire lesson can serve as an embedded assessment. Select lessons in which activities require students to apply significant concepts and skills introduced within the unit. To turn a lesson activity into an assessment, identify the areas of learning and the behaviors that may provide evidence of understanding, and then generate an observation guide or checklist. When a lesson serves as an embedded assessment, your relationship to your students may be more that of an observer than their instructor.

In one lesson of the second-grade Insights unit *Growing Things*, students are asked to work without the teacher's help, if possible. Groups follow written instructions directing them to observe their germinating seedlings, looking for changes since their previous observations, and then individually to record their observations in their science notebooks. At the conclusion of the activity, each group discusses its observations. The teacher's role is described in the teachers' guide:

> An embedded assessment is part of the sequence of learning experiences. As far as students are concerned, Learning Experience 6 seems no different from other lessons. For the teacher, however, there is a role shift. After giving the initial directions, you become an observer—circulating among the groups, carefully observing to assess which skills students have mastered and which skills they still need to work on. Encourage, help and support groups if they need such assistance. (p. 110)

Student Self-Evaluation

Student self-evaluations can be included in the assessment process. They provide unique information to teachers and also encourage self-reflection. Although students may occasionally rate themselves unrealistically high, teachers report that this is not usually the case. In our work, we have found that elementary school students from all over the United States have written candid comments about what they have accomplished, how they think they could improve their work, and which activities they did and did not understand.

While it is possible to construct a self-evaluation form on which children rate themselves in various predetermined areas, open-ended questions that require short written answers about these same areas encourage more reflective responses. Self-evaluation forms should never be presented as tests or graded.

The self-assessments shown in Figures 2–6 and 2–7 ask students to express their opinions about their performance in two formats, a ranking scale and short written answers. In Figure 6–9 on page 128, students rate themselves on the same check sheet used by their teacher.

Self-Evaluation Rating Scale

Name: _____

Date: _____

Directions: Rate yourself. On a scale of one (low) to ten (high), how well did you do each of the following activities?

Constructing ecocolumn

Didn't understand what to do   Made a great one

| 1 | 2 | 3 | 4 | 5 | 6 | 7 | 8 | 9 | 10 |

Observing ecocolumn

Not very often   Every day

| 1 | 2 | 3 | 4 | 5 | 6 | 7 | 8 | 9 | 10 |

Planning the experiment

Had trouble   Well thought-out

| 1 | 2 | 3 | 4 | 5 | 6 | 7 | 8 | 9 | 10 |

Recordkeeping

Did some   Did all

| 1 | 2 | 3 | 4 | 5 | 6 | 7 | 8 | 9 | 10 |

Presentation

Could have tried harder   Did my best

| 1 | 2 | 3 | 4 | 5 | 6 | 7 | 8 | 9 | 10 |

Overall feeling about the *Ecosystems* unit

Liked it a little   Liked it a lot

| 1 | 2 | 3 | 4 | 5 | 6 | 7 | 8 | 9 | 10 |

Things I liked or did well _____

_____

Things I did not like _____

_____

Figure 2-6 *Self-Evaluation Rating Scale from the* STC Ecosystems *unit.**

Self-Evaluation Checklist

Name: _____

Date: _____

Did the chemical tests

Finished some   Finished them all

| | | | | | | | | |

Worked with the materials

Messy   Always careful

| | | | | | | | | |

Recorded and described in charts and notebooks

Wrote a little   Wrote a lot

| | | | | | | | | |

Practiced important safety rules

Some of the time   All of the time

| | | | | | | | | |

Discussed ideas and results with the class

Some of the time   All of the time

| | | | | | | | | |

Worked well with classmates

Some of the time   All of the time

| | | | | | | | | |

Used time well

Wasted time   Worked hard

| | | | | | | | | |

Learned from the unit

Learned a little   Learned a lot

| | | | | | | | | |

Things I liked or did well: _____

_____

Things I did not like: _____

_____

Figure 2-7 *Self-Evaluation Checklist from the* STC Chemical Tests *unit.**

*From the National Science Resources Center's Science and Technology for Children unit entitled *Chemical Tests*, ©1992, National Academy of Sciences, Washington, D.C.

Notebooks and Folders

Student science notebooks have been successfully used for assessment by teachers in all elementary grades, although the amount of information they provide varies with grade level. In lower grades, when students' writing skills are less developed, journals and notebooks are less likely to reflect the extent of their knowledge, since writing may be laborious and difficult (as it may also be for some students in higher grades). Consequently, teachers of lower grades should not expect as much from student notebooks and should collect assessment information in additional ways. In the lower grades it is especially important to encourage students to include drawings and other nonverbal forms of recording in addition to writing.

Open-ended notebook entries, in contrast to forms to complete, allow a student's personal voice to come through. The following sixth grader's journal entry is not likely to appear on any form: "I feel bad about the fish. Because it is like a friend dieing. It is bad because you get atached." And the information in the following fourth grader's journal entries is much richer than that usually collected on a structured observation sheet:

> 11/3/92
>
> Some of the objects—in my mind—behaved very strangely. I expected the glue bottle to sink entierly because it was full and full of a thick substance, but the light, emtey cap held it all up. And the crayon, it floated and I was almost sure it would sink. The only objects that behaved how I had planned were the sicorrs which dropped like a rock and the 2 pencils which both floated. The only difference between the two pencils was one was red and one was normal.

> 11/4/92
>
> I was a little suprised by the marble sinking. I also had excpected the plastic bolt to float. But overall I was pretty acurate in my predictions and guesses. One more thing that suprised me was not having the polyethyline cylinder float. But the one thing I found out that wasn't requiered was attaching. Attaching a floating object to a sinking one made both sink.

If your students are to keep accurate and useful notebooks, they'll need a lot of guidance; a number of helpful guidelines are included in the next chapter. However, if this method doesn't seem worth the effort, you may not want to use it at all.

In addition to narrative writing, science notebooks typically include other, more structured recording formats such as charts, tables, and graphs. While such forms allow fewer possibilities for a student's individual responses to emerge, they are part of scientific communication and can also illustrate learning. Figures 2–8, 2–9, and 2–10 are samples of lab recording sheets currently being used in national curriculum projects. If you provide students with tables for recording information or blank graphs to fill in, consider asking students to construct their own tables and graphs partway through the unit to see whether they understand this scientific form of recording. Elementary school students often correctly draw the axes of a graph but frequently omit labels. Also make sure that your forms include space not only for recording but for reflection.

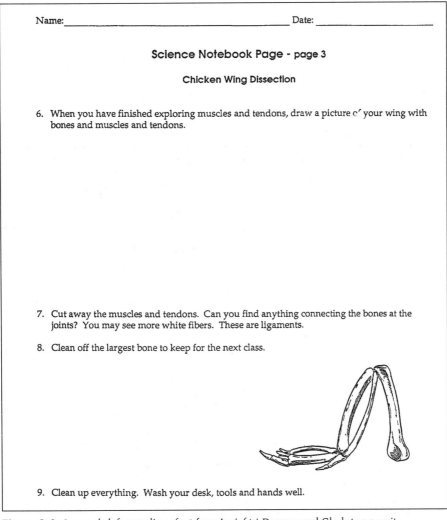

Figure 2-8 *A sample lab recording sheet from* Insights' Bones and Skeletons *unit.*

Name: _____   Date: _____

Science Notebook Page

Animal Skeletons

Similarities and differences between the two skeletons:

Bone Group	Skeleton Number:	Skeleton Number:
Skull		
Arm/Hand		
Leg/Foot		
Pelvis		
Rib Cage		
Vertebral Column		

What do the differences tell you about the animals?

Figure 2-9 *Another sample lab recording sheet from* Insights' *Bones and Skeletons unit.*

Student Swap of Unknown Mixtures   Activity Sheet 10

My Name: _____

Date: June 2, 1992

The unknown mixture is labeled   Abby and Stephanie

What I Did	What Happened
Vinegar	It fizzed + turned yellow.
Red Cabbage Juice	It bubbled and looks like milk.
Iodine	It turned Black
Water	It did the same thing as the Red Cabbage Juice

What I Think It Is	Why I Think So (Give two or more reasons)
Baking soda glum and cornstarch	Because when I put the baking soda Vinegar in It fizzed. And when I put the Iodine in it turned black-purple

Figure 2-10 A *third example of a lab recording sheet from* STC's Chemical Tests *unit.*

Postunit Assessments

Assessments toward the end of a unit may provide sufficient evidence that the students have benefited from classroom activities. Most traditional testing is of this kind. Students take examinations after they have been exposed to the material and have (presumably) learned it. If a teacher's primary concern is that students learn certain content or processes, it may not matter how much they knew to begin with or when the assessment is given, only that they can demonstrate their knowledge and skills. If you have collected sufficient assessment information throughout the unit, it may not be necessary to give a postunit test at all.

The end of the unit is the time to carry out the second half of matched pre/postunit assessments, but it may be more appropriate to use a more complex activity for postunit assessment. For example, having students wire a doll house can be an effective postunit activity in a unit about electricity, but it would hardly be fair as a preunit comparison. As you design your own postunit tests consider allowing your students access to their notebooks if they have kept them; you may want to see if they can use their notes to recall and apply information. Consider designing assessment activities that last more than one class period and take the form of an extended observation or experiment. Several postunit assessment formats are discussed below.

Stations or circuses

Setting up workstations (or "circuses") around the classroom at which individual students perform defined tasks for specific periods of time enables you to:

1. Allow a whole class to do several discrete, hands-on assessment activities in one period.
2. Assess students individually.
3. Anticipate and control what the students will do or see. (For example, you could set up a microscope slide ahead of time and ask students to focus it and draw what they see. Knowing what the focused slide should look like makes assessment easier.)

Tasks can, of course, take different lengths of time; typically each one takes seven to ten minutes, but occasionally one may require as much as twenty minutes. A station assessment from the *Growing Things* unit is included in Figures 2–11a, b, and c.

Name: _____ Date: _____

Growing Things
Final Assessment — Part I

Performance Assessment

Station A

1. Measure and record the height of the two plants in the tray provided by your teacher.

2. Show your recording to your teacher and explain what you think caused one plant to grow more than the other.

Station B

1. Plant the seeds your teacher will give you. Try to remember all the important steps.

2. Now write directions for someone else so that he or she will be able to take care of your plants for the next few weeks.

Figure 2-11a *Page 1 of a station assessment from* Insights' *Growing Things* unit.

Station C

On the tray your teacher will provide, you will see various stages in the germination of a seed and the development of a plant.

1. Show the stages of growth from a dry seed to a full-grown plant by drawing pictures and labeling them in order.

2. Now circle on your pictures those stages — and only those stages — that you can see in the planting tray.

Figure 2-11b *Page 2 of a station assessment from* Insights' *Growing Things* unit.

Station D

Suppose that during one week in class, your group measured its plants and obtained the following measurements in inches.

Plant	Monday inches	Tuesday inches	Wednesday inches	Thursday inches	Friday inches	Monday inches
#1	3	3 1/2	4	5	5 1/2	
#2	1	2	3	4	5	
#3	2	2	3	3	4	
#4	1	3	5	7	9	

1. Construct a graph of the growth of one of the plants.

2. What questions does your graph raise for you?

3. For each plant, what do you think the height will be on Monday? Write your answer in the second column marked Monday.

4. Show your graph to your teacher. Explain your questions, your predictions, and the basis for each.

Figure 2-11c *Page 3 of a station assessment from* Insights' Growing Things *unit.*

Demonstrations

To reduce the time required for assessment you can demonstrate an activity to the whole class and ask them to respond. Depending on your students' ages and your teaching style and objectives, you might want to conduct a whole-class discussion or ask students to respond individually in writing, to questions related to the demonstration. At the end of *Magnets and Motors*, for example, the teacher demonstrates a motor from an earlier lesson and asks students to respond to questions about what they observed.

Data interpretation

You can also give students experimental findings to interpret. This may take the form of:

- Reading and interpreting tables or graphed experimental results.
- Explaining why a set of circumstances occurred.
- Making predictions (see question 4 on the *Electric Circuits* posttest, page 44).

- Using data collected throughout the unit to answer questions. (At the end of the STC *Butterflies* unit, second graders are asked to look over their notebooks and report the number of days it took their chrysalis to hatch.)

Individual experiments (hands-on)

Hands-on assessment activities engage students actively in doing science. For example, as a postunit assessment for STC's *Food Chemistry*, students are given marshmallows and asked to identify their contents by applying the tests (for protein, fat, sugar, and starch) they have learned and used throughout the unit. As a final performance assessment in several electricity units, students are given materials and asked to construct a circuit. In the Insights unit *Bones and Skeletons*, fifth graders are asked to construct a model of the knee using provided materials and to demonstrate how it bends, given the following instructions:

> Your teacher has provided you with craft sticks, thumbtacks, rubber bands, string, cardboard, and glue. If there are other materials available in the classroom that you would like to use, you may ask your teacher for them. Your task is to work in pairs to create a model of the knee and demonstrate to your teacher how it bends when you want it to and allows you to stand up when you want to. (p. 259)

In addition to asking your students to carry out an experiment that you or a curriculum developer has designed, you can ask them to design and perform one of their own.

Stories

Writing stories can be a rich form of final assessment, especially for younger students, allowing them to be creative while incorporating concepts and vocabulary they have learned. Stories can be written as a class or individual activity. In STC's *Organisms* unit, first graders write stories based on their individual and class experiences growing and observing seeds. The story in Figure 2–12 clearly reflects the writer's experience.

Paper-and-pencil tests

Paper-and-pencil tests can be developed for any unit. We recommend that they include open-ended questions and opportunities for drawings and diagrams rather than questions limited to strict recall of factual information. The following three questions are from a postunit assessment for a fourth-grade STC unit, *Floating and Sinking*.

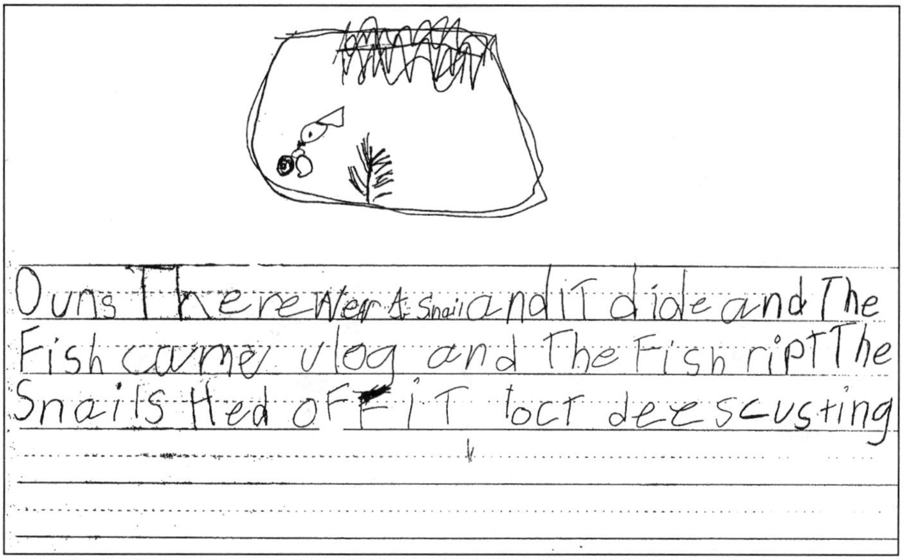

Figure 2-12 *A first grader's postunit story from STC's Organisms unit.*

1. What were three ways you worked with a partner to investigate floating and sinking?
2. What were three things you found out for yourself about the reasons for floating and sinking?
3. What do you want to investigate about floating and sinking?

STC's *Electric Circuits* postunit assessment includes a variety of questions. It's an excellent example of a postunit paper-and-pencil test and is shown in its entirety in Figures 2–13a, b, and c.

All of the California FOSS units include three kinds of postunit assessment—performance, pictorial, and reflective. The sheets in Figures 2–14a, b, and c, taken from the fifth/sixth-grade unit *Variables*, show examples of all three forms.

One of the goals of the STC sixth-grade unit *Ecosystems* is for students to develop an appreciation for the various sides of environmental issues. The assessment focusing on that goal is based on one of two essays that differ in difficulty ("Diapers: An Environmental Problem" and "Oil Fields or a Nature Refuge?"). The teacher's guide contains these instructions:

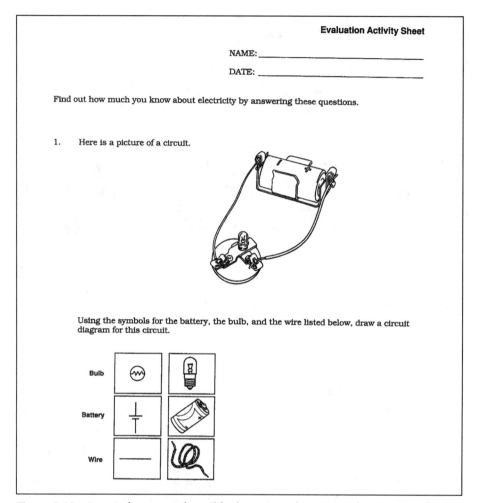

Evaluation Activity Sheet

NAME: _____

DATE: _____

Find out how much you know about electricity by answering these questions.

1. Here is a picture of a circuit.

Using the symbols for the battery, the bulb, and the wire listed below, draw a circuit diagram for this circuit.

Bulb		
Battery		
Wire		

Figure 2-13a *Page 1 of a paper-and-pencil final assessment from STC's Electric Circuits unit.**

You will find two different assessments concerning environmental problems. Each follows a similar format:

- The problem begins with three questions intended to help students focus on the main issues as they read.
- A reading selection describes the problem from different points of view.
- Two questions at the end ask students to take a stand on the issue and then back up their choice with reasons.

*From the National Science Resources Center's Science and Technology for Children unit entitled *Electric Circuits*, ©1991, National Academy of Sciences, Washington, D.C.

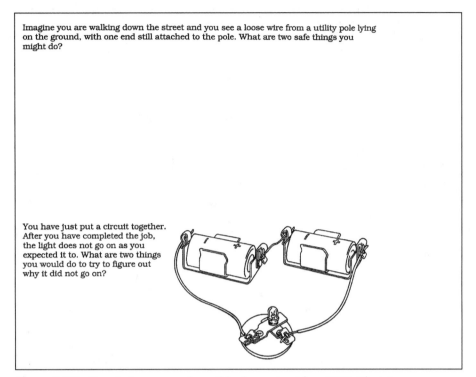

Imagine you are walking down the street and you see a loose wire from a utility pole lying on the ground, with one end still attached to the pole. What are two safe things you might do?

You have just put a circuit together. After you have completed the job, the light does not go on as you expected it to. What are two things you would do to try to figure out why it did not go on?

Figure 2-13b *Page 2 of a paper-and-pencil final assessment from* STC's Electric Circuits *unit.*

The assessments offer you a choice of two degrees of difficulty. . . . You may wish to do the assessments as a whole-class activity, in small groups, or individually. Students can give their responses orally or write them out. Only you know what is most appropriate for your class.

When you evaluate student responses, consider these points:

- Has the student appreciated the complexity of the problem?
- Has the student understood that people can hold widely different but equally valid points on the same problem?
- Did the student list several reasons to back up his or her stand on the issue?

Concept maps, described earlier in this chapter, can also be a form of paper-and-pencil tests. Students can use them as a way to summarize what they know at the end of a course of study.

*From the National Science Resources Center's Science and Technology for Children unit entitled *Electric Circuits,* ©1991, National Academy of Sciences, Washington, D.C.

4. Here are some electrical devices connected by wires and a switch. The bulb is on now. What do you think will happen when the switch is closed?

5. What do you think you learned about electricity this year?

6. What questions do you have about electricity now?

Figure 2-13c *Page 3 of a paper-and-pencil final assessment from* STC's Electric Circuits *unit.**

*From the National Science Resources Center's Science and Technology for Children unit entitled *Electric Circuits,* ©1991, National Academy of Sciences, Washington, D.C.

Name _____   Date _____

FOSS Variables Hands-on Assessment
Student Sheet

Directions: Use the materials at the station to answer the following questions.

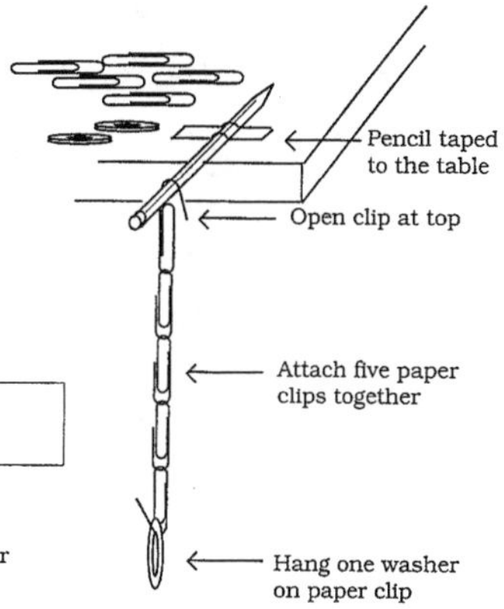

1. Construct a five paper-clip pendulum as shown in the diagram. Use a watch with a second hand to find out how many swings it makes in 10 seconds.

   a. How many swings did it make?

   b. What could you do to make sure that your count is correct?

   _____

   _____

   _____

Pencil taped to the table

Open clip at top

Attach five paper clips together

Hang one washer on paper clip

2. Change the pendulum so that it will swing **a greater number of times** in 10 seconds.

   a. How many washers did you put on the pendulum?

   b. How many paper clips did you use?

   c. Test the pendulum. How many times did it swing in 10 seconds?

   d. How did you know that it would swing more times before you tried it?

   _____

   _____

Figure 2-14a *An example of a hands-on performance assessment from Foss'* Variables *unit.*

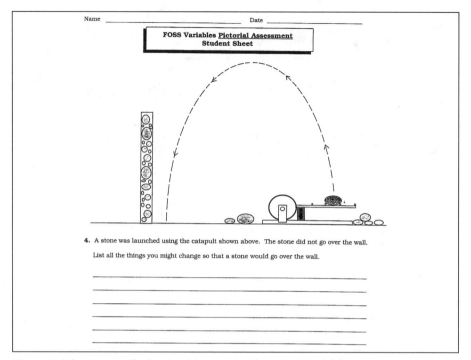

Figure 2-14b *An example of a pictorial assessment from Foss' Variables unit.*

Figure 2-14c *An example of a reflective questions assessment from Foss' Variables unit.*

Assessment that Involves an Audience

Guests

Primary grade teachers often notice that when visitors come to their classrooms the children are very eager to describe what they have learned; they talk spontaneously and answer questions. These teachers are amazed to discover how much their students know—far more than they had imagined. A planned visit from a parent or grandparent, another teacher, the principal, or any other adult provides a relaxed and informal way to assess learning. If you try this approach, have a few stimulating questions ready to throw out to get things started.

Teaching or reporting to others

Some teachers ask their students to teach younger children, to give demonstrations to other classes, or to describe their science activities at a parents night or open house. Presentations like these are a powerful way for children to demonstrate their own learning. You should probably use the *rehearsal* for the public activity as the assessment; that way, any nervousness at the actual event won't hinder an accurate assessment of the students' knowledge. When they make presentations, students have to pull together and organize what they have learned. Presentations based on group effort can require individual students to be responsible for discrete parts, providing an opportunity to assess them separately.

Portfolios

Portfolios are currently used for assessment at state and classroom levels, mostly in the areas of math, art, and writing. The process of generating and keeping portfolios does not differ much from subject to subject and has been well described elsewhere in the professional literature. Although we do not attempt to discuss portfolios in depth in this book, it is important to differentiate portfolios from notebooks and journals and to highlight several of the portfolio's distinguishing features. Portfolios may be more difficult to generate in elementary science than in other subjects because science is taught less often and does not produce as much written material.

Science notebooks generally contain all the written work produced during a unit, semester, or year. In contrast, a portfolio is a *selection* of that work. Who selects the work and the criteria used for selection varies from teacher to teacher. In some classrooms, students make the selection according to criteria established collaboratively between themselves and their teacher. Criteria might be "the piece that was hardest for me to do," "my best piece of work," "the project I learned most from doing," and "a piece that shows important science learning." In other classrooms, the teacher selects work in addition to that chosen by the student. Whatever the system, the portfolio is a selection of work reflecting a deliberate, defined process.

Reflection is an important part of the portfolio process: students often explain orally or in writing why they have made their selections, and these explanations may become a part of the portfolio as well. In some classrooms, teachers interview students about their selections and the interview is added to the portfolio. The portfolio process encourages students to become reflective learners—about what they have done, what was difficult, and what they have learned.

Assessment Systems

This chapter has described and illustrated a number of different assessment approaches. To adequately assess student learning, however, it is important to use a collection, or system, of assessments.

When you are designing assessments for a particular science unit, it is important to include multiple formats, thus increasing the chances that every student will be able to communicate what he or she knows. Develop a collection of assessments that work together and complement each other, keeping the overall goals of the unit in mind. Then check your collection: are there performance assessments, pre/postunit assessments, opportunities for students to talk about what they have done, writing activities (both informal and formal), pencil-and-paper tests, and opportunities for students to make diagrams, maps, and drawings? The assessment systems for two curriculums are presented below as examples.

Electric Circuits

This curriculum for grades five and six is a sixteen-lesson unit with a range of suggested assessment activities. The numbers refer to the lessons in the unit, and boldface indicates those activities that also serve as the more formal assessments.

> 1. **Draw a light bulb (pre).** Try to light a bulb using a battery and wires and draw your attempts.

2. **List what you know about electricity and would like to learn (groups).**
3. **Fill out prediction sheets and then check predictions using materials for various battery-bulb-connectors arrangements.**
4. After working with the materials, draw a light bulb in a circuit.
5. Fill out a **prediction sheet** again, build a circuit and make a drawing of it.
6. Build a circuit tester, fill out a **prediction sheet**.
7. Explore conductors and insulators.
8. **Draw light bulbs** after dissecting one (**post**).
9. Draw hidden circuits in a mystery box.
10. Draw circuit diagram in notebook (learned symbols).
11. Draw series and parallel circuits.
12. **Plan for a flashlight.**
13. **Build a flashlight.**
14–16. **Plan for, wire, and draw an electrical system for a doll house.**

Electric Circuits ends with a number of suggested **postunit assessment instruments** (no teacher is expected to do them all). Students can be asked to:

1. Write what they know about electricity.
2. Create a display.
3. Build and then draw a circuit (specified parts).
4. Use a circuit tester to work out the wiring in a hidden circuit box.
5. Complete a paper-and-pencil assessment [see Figures 2–14a, b, and c].
6. Keep notebooks: these include all work sheets, drawings, diagrams, and plans and are reviewed by the teacher.

A teacher checklist describes skills, program products, and behaviors to watch for as an observational guide.

In summary, the assessment system for this unit includes drawings, prediction sheets, pre/postactivities about light bulbs and electricity, products, an embedded lesson (doll house), a hands-on posttest, and a paper-and-pencil posttest. In addition, student notebooks and a checklist tied to objectives are also used.

Plant Growth and Development

In the following list of lessons from STC's second-grade unit *Plant Growth and Development*, boldface indicates those activities that also serve as the more formal assessments. Bear in mind that all written observations and graphs of data also provide assessment information.

1. **Two preunit assessments: discuss what students know about plants and would like to know (content); observe a seed using hand lens, and record (skills).**

2. Students dissect, observe and draw soaked seeds and embryos.

3. Students plant FastPlant® seeds.

4. Students thin and transplant seedlings.

5. Students begin measuring and graphing plant growth in centimeters: teacher informally assesses measurement skills.

6. Students observe leaves and flower buds and record.

7. Students observe and record growth spurt for seven days, predicting next day's growth each day.

8. **Prelesson assessments: drawing of what a bee looks like, and class discussion about what they know about bees.**

9. Students observe dead bees and make bee sticks used for pollinating flowers.

10. Students use hand lens to observe and record flower morphology over a week.

11. Students spend a week pollinating their flowers.

12. Students observe pod formation and measure and graph plant growth.

13. **Students make large models of the *Brassica* flower.**

14. **Students make bee models and then act out pollination using bee and flower.**

15. **Students answer questions about two given graphs; teacher assesses ability to read, interpret, and identify elements of graphs.**

16. Students harvest seeds.

A Teacher's Record Chart provides a checklist of student products, skills, and knowledge to note during observations.

Postunit Assessments:

1. Students sequence *Brassica rapa* life-cycle cards.
2. Students make a postunit drawing of a bee.
3. Students complete a pre/postunit assessment of their knowledge by adding to (and subtracting from) their list of what they know about plants.

In summary, this unit combines pre/postassessments on plants and bees (discussions and drawing), two performance assessments (building a plant model, role-playing pollination), a graph interpretation assessment, and a postunit pictorial sequencing activity about the life cycle of FastPlants®. In addition, whether or not the plants thrive and produce seeds provides an assessment of how well students took care of them and how successfully the flowers were pollinated. Student notebooks and an observational checklist tied to objectives complete this system.

Conclusion

The number and sorts of formal assessments you use will be influenced by the material you are teaching, the age and experience of your students, and your efforts to include assessments that reach all students. You may be fortunate enough to have a curriculum that provides active assessments, and need to add only a few additional ones. If you are designing your own assessments, you can refer to the different formats presented in this chapter to put together a collection that engages your students and provides you with the evidence of their learning that you require.

Managing Assessments

· ◆ ·

In traditional assessment, typically, all students are given the identical paper-and-pencil test. The newer assessments are "messier": they may combine several different formats; they often use or generate materials that are hard to file and store; and students may not carry out the same assessment activity at the same time. You need to coordinate the different assessment techniques, personally observe each student carry them out, and make sure that your assessments cover all content areas. This means you have to be clear about what you are doing and proceed systematically. You also need to be able to describe and defend your actions: communicating your changes in assessment approach to the rest of the school community in a way that addresses their questions and concerns is key. The following suggestions may help you make the transition more easily.

Managing the Transition

Start small

Don't throw out your traditional tests immediately. Instead, redesign your assessment program gradually, perhaps adding one new technique— a pre/postunit assessment or an embedded assessment, for example— to a single science unit. In the beginning treat the new assessments as "extras." Then, as both you and your school community become more familiar with alternative assessment, increase the number you incorporate into your instructional methods. Remember that it will take more than a year for you to make a complete transition.

If your school district has adopted a hands-on science curriculum completely or partially made up of science kits, some of them may have alternative assessments built in; this will limit the number of assessments you need to develop on your own. However, if your units are developed locally and don't include any active assessments, look at some of the new NSF-sponsored curriculums we mentioned in Chapter 1 for ideas. The examples in this book will also be helpful.

Be realistic

To help ensure that your assessment techniques will be well received and supported, base them on activities your school community values: there should be a realistic fit. For example, it will be easier to use student science notebooks and journals as assessment vehicles in a district or a school in which the writing process is taught and students write routinely than in one that places little emphasis on writing.

Introducing journals in a school where writing is not emphasized means you will need to spend time helping students to feel comfortable with the process. At first their science journals may not yield much information useful for assessment. But if they have continuing opportunities to write both in science and in other subjects, their ability to express themselves in written form will increase. In time their written work will more accurately reflect their knowledge and will be more useful for assessment.

If writing is not emphasized in your school, it is important to supplement it with other forms of assessment, such as drawing and oral presentations. Use your judgment: if your students have science only one hour a week, science notebooks may help them bridge the long time between classes. However, you may prefer to use that writing time for other science activities.

If your district places great emphasis on graded report cards, it is especially important that you be able to translate your assessment criteria into traditional grades. All the assessments described in this book can be used to generate grades (see Chapter 6 on scoring). Translating student achievement measured through active assessment into a single letter or number diminishes its value, but can be done.

Find someone to work with

Try to find a colleague, preferably teaching at your grade level, who is also interested in active assessment. If you are lucky enough to be teaching the same science unit at the same time, you can help each other develop and manage assessment materials and interpret student work. The scoring rubric for traditional tests unequivocally separates right and wrong answers; interpreting student work in active assessments is more complex. The work is richer and usually open to a variety of interpretations. Also, what is being assessed, such as the evolution of a student's skill or her conceptual knowledge, may be less clear cut. As you develop criteria for judging and interpreting student work and then apply those criteria, you may benefit from a second opinion. A colleague may also suggest discussion questions that will prompt you to describe your learning goals and help you identify ways to assess them. For developing any specific assessment techniques and activities, two heads are definitely better than one.

Don't increase your workload

Don't add to your workload if you can help it. Your goal is not to create a second tier of tests in addition to what you are already doing or to develop assessments that require extra time from you or your students. Using embedded assessments should free time previously required for a midunit test, for example.

Nevertheless, the transition period will probably require some added time and effort. Remember that the additional time required to carry out the new active assessments will reward you: you will understand your students better and be able to plan better teaching strategies. Keeping a couple of things in mind may help you maintain a manageable workload.

First, everything that goes on in your classroom can provide evidence of your students' thinking and learning. Therefore, you don't need to design all your new assessments from scratch. Look for things that you do routinely that could fit into your assessment scheme. Take advantage of activities like preunit discussions that are already in place in your science unit. An ongoing activity that you and your students already prepare for and perform can be specifically designated as an assessment, one that will not disrupt the classroom work as traditional tests do. Activities in which students produce materials that demonstrate that they can apply what they know are obvious choices. Many teachers also conclude units by asking students to prepare a presentation or a display, perhaps for a younger grade or a parents night. Your own recorded observations of student activities are equally valid: focused observation is a form of assessment.

Second, make your assessments serve multiple purposes. Just as ongoing activities can double as assessments, a single activity can be used to assess multiple goals. Select activities that will provide you with as much information about student learning as possible—activities that encourage students to pull together science content, skills, and processes. If you use portfolios or other written materials to assess science learning, use them to assess language arts simultaneously.

Managing the Logistics

In the active assessment of hands-on science programs, several activities often take place simultaneously and produce a variety of outcomes—products, drawings, and other unwieldy items. Unless you approach them systematically, both the program and the assessments can become overwhelming. The following general guidelines can help:

- Date everything. Student work, unless it is bound, often ends up as a nonchronological jumble, so dates are essential.

- Separate assessments you plan to keep from work that gets passed back. Find a place to store the ongoing collection, perhaps using a separate folder for each child. You may earmark particular lab reports or specific notebook entries for assessment, and it may not always be possible for you to set these aside, but note what they are and how you intend to use them. You can hang file folders in boxes and invite children to file their own work. Use different envelopes for weekly work that goes home. Drawers work well for storage if you have them. If possible, take photographs of three-dimensional products to put in student folders, and send the originals home.

- Make sure your custodial staff know what you are saving and what they may remove.

- Keep learning objectives clear. Student enthusiasm and interest, often high, can distract you from the assessment question of whether and what students have learned.

There are also a number of more specific logistical issues related to individual assessment techniques.

Pre/postunit assessments

It is particularly important that students do not see their preunit assessment efforts until after the postunit assessment has been completed. If you give your students a sheet of paper with three headings, "What I know," "What I want to know," and "What I learned" (the KWL chart), they will respond to the first two statements at the start of the unit and then have to list what they have learned on the same sheet of paper at its finish. This means they will be able to look back and forth between the columns and adjust their responses. Therefore, if you plan to have this activity serve as a matched pre/postunit assessment, the students will need to enter their postunit responses on a different sheet of paper. It may also be important to elicit the preunit responses before any other activities related to the unit are begun.

However, pre/postunit assessments do not need to be limited to the beginning and end of a curriculum unit; they can also be used for subtopics within the unit. (The same guidelines apply, of course.)

If your pre/postunit assessments require students to write or draw, then using different-colored paper for the pre and post portions makes them easily distinguishable even if the two piles get confused.

Embedded assessments

These present few management issues, because they occur within regular instruction. You do need to decide whether to tell students that the activity (or lesson) is being used for assessment. Some teachers don't share this information with students. Many of those who do also involve their students in the generation of criteria for judging performances.

Class charts

Sometimes teachers display class-generated charts and lists, such as "What we know" or "What we want to find out," and then add to them throughout the course of the unit. Using a different color each time makes it easy to keep track of the original, preunit entries and the stages at which successive entries appeared. Some teachers identify each comment by date and note the student who contributed it.

Notebooks

Students have to learn how to keep notebooks as well as how to write about scientific investigations. At first they may do an inadequate job on both tasks. They may skip entries, they may not write completely about their observations, they may forget to date their pages or title their graphs. However, they will be practicing the skills they need to improve in order to keep good notebooks in the future. These notebooks may not be accurate reflections of what they know, but they are not a waste of time. All of this practice is a part of developing scientific literacy.

If you ask your students to keep science notebooks, the following guidelines may be useful:

- Ask students to date everything.
- Have them place the pages in looseleaf notebooks in chronological order.
- Limit entries to one per page; the notebooks will be easier to read.

- Provide adequate time for writing. Younger children write slowly; older children may have a great deal they want to include.

- If some or all of your students are emerging writers, consider dictation; some teachers arrange for less skilled students to dictate to a classmate.

- Give students time to organize their notebooks. Just a few minutes each science period may be adequate.

- Be clear about what papers you expect to go into the notebook.

- Establish clear procedures for where students should leave notebooks and when you will look at them.

- If you give students questions to respond to as they write, ask them to copy the questions into their notebooks. Otherwise the notebooks may contain incomplete thoughts and yes/no responses and will be more difficult to analyze. When asking students to give reasons or explanations for events, ask them to give two or three; this seems to encourage deeper thinking. (In Great Britain, the Assessment of Performance Unit routinely asked students to provide three reasons.)

- Ask students to include drawings, plans, predictions, maps, graphs, tables, and charts in addition to written narrative.

- Ask students to write conclusions to experiments explaining the meaning of their data. Too often students only report findings, leaving you to wonder if and how they interpreted them. (This is a difficult task and takes a lot of practice. You may need to model it for your class.)

- If you use lab sheets (which do help students organize data), leave plenty of room for large script and large drawings.

- Think of juicy questions that invite reflection and speculation: What surprised you about your investigations today? Why do you think your results are different from your partner's? What might be contaminating your results?

- Challenge your students to write up lab procedures so that someone else could follow them.

- If you use a curriculum that contains checklists on which to record work completed or learning goals attained, staple a copy of the checklist in each student notebook. That way they can participate in the checking-off process.

- Help students understand the purpose for keeping notebooks: What should they put down, and why? for whom? Are students' notebooks the same as scientists'? Find opportunities to ask students to use their notebooks. Ask them to look back over observations and investigations in order to answer specific questions. Tell them at the beginning of the unit that they will be using their notes at the end (to write a report, answer questions, or prepare a presentation). This may encourage them to keep more complete records. Also remember that incomplete and unreadable notebooks do not mean that students have not done the work or do not understand what they have done.

- For your students who have difficulty writing (they are too young, their language arts skills are inadequate or undeveloped, English is their second language), rely on other forms of assessment.

- Model writing up a lab report. Show your students the process of making corrections and additions. Indicate when it is appropriate and useful to include a graph and explain what supporting information should accompany it. Remember that scientific writing is different from other writing they may have done.

- Make a point of reading your students' notebooks, even if infrequently. Add written comments if you possibly can; this shows you value the notebooks. It helps to establish a regular schedule. Some teachers read and comment on a few notebooks each week, thus covering the entire class over a period of time. (Figures 3–1 and 3–2 are notebook pages on which the students' teachers have shared their evaluation criteria.)

Checklists

Many teachers find that checklists make them feel secure—they are reassured that they are "covering all the bases" and observing everything they intend. If you feel overwhelmed sorting through the wealth of observational data you collect, checklists can help you organize this information.

Design your checklists to reflect what you consider to be the important skills, processes, attitudes, and content in any science unit. (Some teachers ask their students to help identify the important learning areas.) You may want to itemize the different products, worksheets, and other materials you expect your students to complete; you will then be able to make sure you observe each of your students in each area you have defined.

Figure 3-1 A page from a student notebook, with the teacher's narrative comments, from STC's Ecosystems unit.

Some checklists provide limited recording space, just enough for a check mark. This does not allow you to record comments about how or what students are doing, how they are developing and changing, or how concepts or skills have taken hold and evolved. A checklist with only a few student names per page or that provides space for observations allows you to make narrative comments.

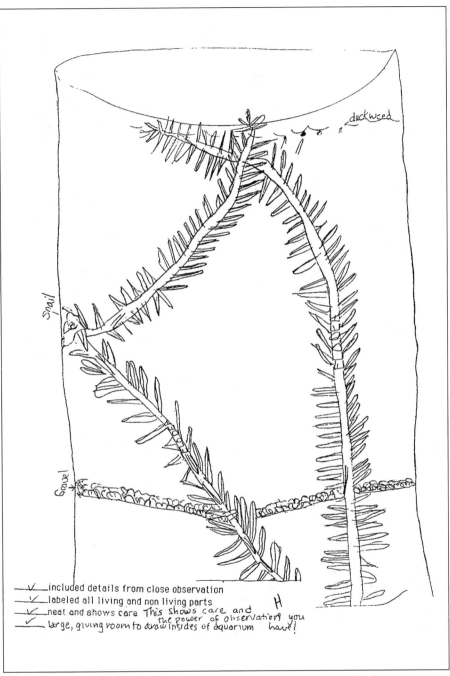

Figure 3-2 Another page from a student notebook. This teacher used a checklist from STC's Ecosystems unit to evaluate the entry.

Student/Class Profiles: Scientific Concepts *Growing Things*					
Name/Group #	Function of Seeds	Recognition of Seeds Parts	Stages of Germination and of Growth	Recognition of Roots, Stem, Leaves	Function of Roots, Stem

Figure 3-3 *This checklist from* Insights' Growing Things *unit captures a lot of information for a number of students but has limited space for teachers' comments.*

Some checklists include space for both the student and the teacher to record opinions (see Figure 6–9 on page 128). These are useful in student-teacher conferences.

Figures 3–3, 3–4, and 3–5, are examples of several kinds of checklists.

Photographs

Keeping track of children's activities while they work can be difficult and storing the sometimes bulky products of their science activities may be impossible. Photographs taken of students as they perform experiments and investigations serve as excellent reminders of what the students were doing, whom they worked with, and how they handled equipment. Photographs also provide a visual record of student products that cannot be stored.

Teacher's Record Chart of Student Progress for *Floating and Sinking*--Learning Goals

Student: _____   Class: _____

LEARNING GOALS	Checklist	OBSERVATIONS
Using Instruments • Uses a spring scale to measure force • Uses a graduated cylinder to measure changes in water level		
Identifying Properties • Observes that submerged objects cause a change in the water level • Observes that objects appear to weigh less in water • Observes that water has weight • Observes that salt mixes with water to form saltwater • Observes that saltwater exerts a greater floating force on objects than fresh water does		
Collecting, Recording, and Interpreting Data • Makes and tests predictions • Organizes data and uses it to make predictions		
Specific Goals • Constructs a floating shape out of clay • Constructs clay cylinders that are the same size and shape as cylinders made of other materials		

Figure 3-4 *This checklist from the* STC *unit* Floating and Sinking *provides some space for narrative comments.**

*From the National Science Resources Center's Science and Technology for Children unit entitled *Floating and Sinking*, ©1992, National Academy of Sciences, Washington, D.C.

Teacher's Record Chart of Student Progress for *Ecosystems*

	Student
PRODUCTS Lesson 1: Notebook: individual pre-test	
Bottles: cleaned, bases and labels removed	
Lesson 2: Notebook: answers to questions about water plants	
Bottles: marked and cut	
Lesson 3: Aquarium set up: gravel, water, and plants	
Activity Sheet 1	
Lesson 4: Aquarium set up: snails and guppies	
Activity Sheet 2	
Lesson 5: Notebook: producer/consumer relationships	
Lesson 6: Terrarium set up: soil, seeds, rock, leaf litter, twig	
Activity Sheet 3	
Lesson 7: Terrarium set up: crickets and isopods	
Activity Sheet 4	
Lesson 8: Notebook: how the terrarium can affect the aquarium	
Lesson 9: List of human-made pollutants	
Notebook: list of human-made pollutants	
Lesson 10: Activity Sheet 5	
Lesson 11: Activity Sheet 6	
Lesson 13: Activity Sheet 7	
Lesson 14: Contributes to team's experiment report	
Contributes to class data list and conclusions	
Lesson 15: Activity Sheet 8	
Lesson 16: Presentation on the Chesapeake Bay	
Notebook: reflective writing	
LEARNING GOALS Can construct ecocolumn from soda bottles	
Can set up terrarium and aquarium	
Handles living organisms appropriately	
Exhibits sensitivity for living things	
Understands concept of plants as producers and animals as consumers	
Can make predictions based on information and experience	
Can make valid comparisons of different plants, animals, ecosystems	
Can read and interpret the pH scale	
Understands that environmental problems are complex and that their solutions involve trade-offs	
Can analyze experimental data, and base conclusions on data. Understands reasons for discrepant results	
GENERAL SKILLS Follows directions	
Records observations with drawings or words	
Works cooperatively	
Contributes to discussions	

Figure 3-5 A *"check-mark only"* checklist from STC's Ecosystems unit. *The distinction between "Products," "Learning Goals," and "General Skills" provides a useful framework.**

*From the National Science Resources Center's Science and Technology for Children unit entitled *Ecosystems*, ©1992, National Academy of Sciences, Washington, D.C.

Assessment Strategies

Assessing individuals in paired or group activities

In most, if not all, of the new science curriculums, students are expected to work in pairs or small groups. It can be a challenge to assess individual students. The following approaches may help:

- Occasionally ask students within the group to work independently, either in making something or planning and carrying out an experiment.

- Ask students to assess themselves. (A teacher we know asks her students what they would do differently tomorrow: "It gives me food for thought for my observation notes and I can say, 'I am glad you are carrying through on your goals.' I also ask them what they would want me to do differently tomorrow. They are very honest, and it helps me plan my work.")

- Ask individual team members to be responsible for specific segments of the group assignment. This will work only in certain situations. In STC's *Electric Circuits* unit, teams of students are directed to wire "houses" made from cardboard cartons. One teacher who used the unit asked each student to wire a separate room. Once the project was complete, students individually diagrammed their wiring schemes.

- Ask each student to write up the process he or she went through as a team member in making an object or carrying out an investigation.

- Hold individual conferences or interviews to assess each student's understanding and knowledge. These do not need to be long— five minutes can give you plenty of information—and you can pull children out for interviews while other science activities are going on. Some teachers enlist the help of parents, aides, or student teachers. Some teachers interview students during recess; others interview students throughout the day, not just during science period. Students generally look forward to these interviews and don't mind missing recess or anything else for this opportunity. Although the logistics may be difficult, teachers with class sizes over thirty have successfully interviewed all their students. Bear in mind that individual interviews may be something you carry out only two or three times a year.

- If your students are not comfortable in a one-to-one situation, or if you need to save time, interview two students together. You will still be able to assess each child adequately. Respond to your students' levels of comfort.

- Hold group interviews. One teacher we know calls them science clubs, and describes them as discussion groups. Either the teacher or a student posts a discussion topic for which students sign up. Listening to the group discuss an idea can be a very useful form of assessment. If discussion groups appeal to you, be aware that students will need to learn how to do this, and you may need to model questions and responses.

Observation notes

Teacher observation is central to assessing hands-on science but is often hard to manage systematically. It is important to establish procedures for carrying out and recording observations that ensure that important content, attitudes, skills, and procedures are observed for each student. Remember three basic rules:

1. Keep it short and simple.
2. Record only what you see; don't interpret.
3. Don't trust your memory; write it down.

Here are some approaches that have worked for others:

- Keep a folder for each child into which you put observations and anecdotal information.

- Write observations on computer labels that have been printed with individual student names. Later stick them in a notebook in which you've designated separate pages for each child. (Regular blank peel-off labels are an alternative.) As a variation, print science topics about which you want to collect observational data on the labels and write in students' names and your observations.

- Record observations on index cards and then file them.

- Make up a checklist with each child's name and the areas/lessons you plan to observe, leaving space to record as extensively as you wish (a check mark, comments, longer narrative).

- Observe and take notes on only one or two groups or three or four individual students per class period, gradually getting around to everyone.

Questioning

In assessment it is often appropriate for a teacher to take on the role of "silent observer," noting what students do and say spontaneously. But a more active role, questioning to explore students' thinking and finding out how well they can explain what they are doing, is also compatible with assessment. The particular role you take at any time depends to some extent on your teaching style and on your students and to a larger extent on what you are trying to assess. Good questioning takes practice; using open-ended questions and giving students time to think before they respond will elicit the best answers.

Managing Public Relations with Administrators and Parents

Build your case

If you are going to legitimize what you're doing within your school system, it is important to articulate your assessment system clearly. Ideally, a teacher's assessment efforts will have the full support of the administration, especially the science supervisors or principal (not always the case!). And even with that support, individual teachers still need to be able to explain their actions to students and their parents. To do this effectively:

- Know your instructional goals and objectives.
- Know how you intend to assess them.
- Know the criteria you will use to review student work.
- Make sure that the assessments cover all students and all areas.

During the transition in your assessment practices, it helps to be more formal than you might otherwise be in establishing and maintaining your assessment data. This will help you when you need to describe your assessment activities to your principal, other teachers, students, and parents.

Politics

Building support for alternative science assessment is like building support for any new program. People need to see the techniques in action, perhaps try them out themselves, and be told how they are administered and interpreted. Resist the temptation to carry out your first attempts in secrecy. Invite the curious and the skeptical to your room to see what is going on. Build up a collection of sample student assessments you can show to the principal or to parents during conferences. Collect actual student work (but remove the students' names) so you can use them freely to educate a diverse audience. Matched pre/postunit assessments that provide evidence of clear growth are compelling examples of successful active assessments.

Parents

Often teachers send parents a letter explaining what students will be doing in school and what they may be bringing home. Consider sending parents a letter about the new assessments you will be using, taking this opportunity to build support for your efforts. It is important to establish that this is a legitimate, respected movement within the national education community, not your own venture or experiment with inadequate backing or educational context. An initial letter to parents also demonstrates that you are not trying to hide anything. Including the following points should reassure most parents:

- There is both national and international interest in active assessment.
- Active assessments are being used in increasing numbers of school districts all over the United States.
- Active assessment is an equitable way to assess student learning.
- Through active assessment educators expect to assess more validly what we consider scientific learning than has been possible using standardized tests.
- Active assessments look different from other tests with which parents are familiar. (Describe one or two.)

In addition, tell parents how you plan to grade their child. If you mention teacher observation, student involvement, or student notebooks, include the specific criteria you have developed to evaluate these factors.

To increase parents' exposure to alternative assessments and encourage them to review their child's work, send home written assessments, journals, projects, videos of student performances, or other work related to assessment, and ask parents to sign and return them.

An interactive workshop in which parents do hands-on activities is another way to educate them about active assessments. Explain what you look for as you watch students work and demonstrate how you keep track of this information using, for example, an observation checklist.

Many new assessments are performance based, which means that students are assessed on the way in which they carry out their science work.

Drawing parallels to other areas in which performance review is used, such as sports, business, and music, may help parents understand how you assess students.

Some teachers bring parents into the assessment process during parent-student-teacher conferences. Parents, students, and teachers all examine the student's work and comment on it. Together they set goals for the next marking period based on the assessments. Although ideally each party should feel equal to the others in this process, this may take time to develop.

Conclusion

Every classroom is unique, and every teacher has her or his own way of organizing and managing materials, children, and curriculum. Hands-on science brings with it a number of challenges: products and materials must be stored, objects need to be handled, children must be organized into groups and allowed to move about the classroom in an orderly atmosphere. Most teachers find that the classroom management issues decrease in importance as they gain experience with inquiry teaching.

Most of the guidelines for managing active assessment in a materials-based science classroom are natural extensions of the management issues related to the science classroom itself. If a teacher is comfortable with a hands-on science curriculum, the inclusion of the active assessments does not pose an additional burden.

FOUR

Curriculum Developers Talk About Assessment

• ◆ •

Here's my advice to people who are going to sit down and lay out assessments for a certain curriculum. I really think you need to have a solid understanding of where kids are in their growth in terms of their thinking skills, what they're capable of, and their work skills. Once you have a handle on where they are developmentally, look at the curriculum—look for activities and experiences that you feel will give the children enough richness so that an assessment at that point would give you a lot of feedback. Look at your goals for the unit—what is it that you want the children to get out of it? Really pinpoint what's important for you to assess.
WENDY BINDER, *National Science Resources Center*

Active assessments can be used to assess student learning of single, specific concepts or skills and student comprehension of an entire curriculum, although the latter goal usually requires a coordinated set of assessments. How can a teacher design a series of assessments that reveals what she needs to know about student learning?

Curriculum developers, like classroom teachers who are designing assessments, grapple with this and related issues, such as what to assess, how many assessments to use, where to place them within the unit, and which formats to use. Developers of national curriculums follow one of four approaches: to provide no assessments, to offer assessments only at the end of the unit, to embed assessments throughout the lessons, or to offer assessments that can be used flexibly by teachers. The third approach is probably most applicable to the classroom teacher who must formulate assessments for an entire unit.

This chapter draws on conversations with three curriculum developers—one whose assessments are used flexibly by teachers and two who develop embedded assessment systems—about decisions they make. We hope you find their experiences, dilemmas, and solutions illuminating.

Kathy Daiker is a curriculum developer for the Full Option Science System (FOSS). Each FOSS module offers three forms of assessments that address the major ideas covered in the lessons. Kathy describes the assessments for a grade-five/six module published in 1992. Although the assessments appear at the end of the module, the teacher's guide suggests they may be used whenever a teacher wants to know more about what students have learned. Wendy Binder and David Hartney describe assessments for a grade-one and a grade-four curriculum, respectively; these units were developed as part of the Science and Technology for Children (STC) series, sponsored by the National Science Resources Center.

Each of our three authorities first describes the unit, then discusses the issues considered in formulating the assessments, and finally comments on how the final assessment system reflects the unit's instructional goals.

These curriculum developers begin by teaching their intended lessons (trial teaching), and then write a draft of the curriculum that is taught by teachers across the country (field testing). In their comments the developers refer to the trial-teaching phase of curriculum development.

The Three Curriculum Units

Kathy's four-lesson module is called *Variables* and is for grades five and six. She summarizes it this way:

> In the *Variables* unit the main goal is for students to learn the process of doing a controlled experiment. Students build pendulums, paper-cup lifeboats, popsicle-stick airplanes, and mini-catapults. Each activity runs a parallel course asking students to set up a standard system and change one variable at a time to see how it affects the outcome. Students learn the importance of changing one variable at a time.

Wendy's sixteen-lesson unit, *Organisms*, is for first grade. As she describes it,

> Children investigate a variety of plants and animals and, through their observations, class discussions, and activities, arrive at their own criteria for describing plants and animals, directly leading to how plants

and animals are alike and how they are different. These comparisons help children discover that there are needs basic to most organisms and needs specific to individual organisms.

Floating and Sinking is a sixteen-lesson unit for fourth grade. According to David,

> *Floating and Sinking* is about kids trying to figure out why some things float and some things sink in water. I want them to have productive experiences with the interaction between water and the things we put in it. And, I hope that the kids who understand water will extend that to other liquids, such as salt water, which is a big part of this unit. If they understand it for both water and salt water, and have found ways to answer their own questions, then they have attained the top expectation of the unit.

Predesigning Considerations

Identify learning goals

Developing meaningful assessments requires a clear understanding of what a particular science unit is about, which activities are central to it, and what students are expected to learn. The learning goals may be broad—an appreciation for living things—or specific—how to use a microscope and make three kinds of slides. The important thing is to define these learning goals clearly so that the assessments can address them. This direct connection between instruction and assessment makes it possible to measure what you consider educationally significant. All three developers spoke about this process. Wendy's overall suggestion is:

> Look at your goals for the unit—what it is that you want the children to get out of it and what you feel you want your assessment to check. Do you want them all to be able to use a certain measurement tool, or is that incidental to the big picture? Really pinpoint what's important that you want to assess. You don't have to assess everything.

Clarifying learning goals is often difficult. Talking them through with someone who asks questions and pushes for clear definitions is one effective way to make it easier. Wendy and David explain their curriculum goals and instructional and assessment strategies to each other as they work, relying on each other's insights. At FOSS, Kathy says, "We never do anything alone. There is always a group of developers, and often teachers, working together."

Each curriculum developer's learning goals shaped the subsequent assessments. Wendy describes her learning goals this way:

> I want children to gain an awareness of the diversity of life. Focusing on plants and animals, I hope the children discover that there are basic needs that most living things have in order to live and be healthy, and that plants and animals have certain characteristics in common, such as the fact that they grow and change, as well as individual characteristics. I want them to develop positive attitudes and a sensitivity toward living things, and to be able to care for an animal or plant over a period of time. I also want to help them realize the relevance of living things in their lives and that they also are a living thing.

David's goals for *Floating and Sinking* and Kathy's for *Variables* are more concrete and specific, frequently the case when curriculums focus on investigations of physical science. David says:

> A major goal for the unit is for students to learn that weight alone does not determine whether an object will float or sink. Another 'big idea' is that the relative weight of the liquid has an effect on how well an object floats. Learning that making and testing predictions is a useful process is another major goal for students.

Kathy's goals are similarly specific:

> The big idea we want kids to learn in *Variables* is how to do a controlled experiment, so the process is more important here than the content. That's why you see no consistency in the content of the four lessons—it is the process of doing the controlled experiments that matters.

Looking over all three developers' learning goals it is evident that some are more concrete than others and therefore easier to assess. For example, Wendy's goal of helping the students "realize the relevance of living things in their lives" is harder to assess than Kathy's learning "how to do a controlled experiment." But every goal does not need to be assessed. Once your learning goals are set, you need to choose which will be assessed and which will not. Attitudes and global concepts, for example, are very hard to assess, and are often best approached through teacher observation, if they are assessed at all.

Note that Wendy and David articulate both general and specific goals. Don't be afraid to set broad, large-scale goals for children as well as more concrete ones. One advantage to a system of assessments with several forms is that it is possible to determine whether or not children have achieved these larger, often instrumental goals, not just the specific ones.

Review developmental considerations

The intended grade level for a unit further defines which assessments are developmentally appropriate. For example, written assessments work well only with older children, although even some of them still communicate better in a nonwritten format. Panel discussions and debates are particularly appropriate for sixth graders, since only at this grade level do children have some capacity for understanding that there can be equally compelling arguments on all sides of an issue; younger children have difficulty taking different points of view.

Wendy talks at some length about developmental considerations:

> At this age, six going on seven, their thinking is becoming less centered on themselves and beginning to be affected by others. They can observe, they can use their senses, but it's not particularly refined. I'm having them do a lot of observing and comparing so I am very interested in where they are with that. Children at this level can begin to compare and contrast, but while some of the children in first grade can look at only one characteristic of an object and compare it with another, others can look at more than one. There will be a wide range in that classroom, and I need to take that into consideration.

Drawings can be powerful assessment tools with young children. Although drawings can also be useful with older children, their hesitations about drawing and "getting it wrong" may get in the way. It's always a good idea to ask students to write a sentence under their drawings, since pictures often require written comments to explain the thoughts behind them more fully. Ask those students who cannot write explanations to show you their drawings and explain them, or have them dictate their explanations to someone else. Student drawings and explanations can be collected and turned into a class book. Wendy used drawings extensively for assessment in *Organisms*:

> Children at this age are drawing a lot. They're beginning to write in sentences, some not as well as others, depending on the period of the year. A lot of the assessments that are written will be pictures with one or two sentences, or very simple sheets on which they list descriptive words.

Discussion is another central way to assess young children. Wendy relied on it to assess students' understanding of their experiences growing seeds:

> Language experience in first grade is imperative for one type of assessment. I had two points in the unit where I sat down with the class and got them talking about what they had just done. For one we sat

down in a group and I said, "What if we were going to tell another first grade class or your parents what we did with seeds and what we learned?" I started them off: "What did we do to find out about the seeds?" They said, "We planted them." I said, "What did we have to do to plant them?" My questions prompted them to recap what we did and then add what we learned about it. It was a way for them to report and me to record. I really view that as an assessment.

Some scientific skills and processes, such as observing, developing hypotheses, and designing experiments, are manifested differently at different ages. Since the educational and research communities have little understanding of how these skills develop, teachers and curriculum developers must depend on their own experience and their knowledge of their students' capacities to determine how to assess them. Although *Floating and Sinking* contains many opportunities for students to plan and carry out experiments, David limited the assessments because most children in fourth grade are not developmentally ready to design their own experiments. As he says,

> I didn't feel it was appropriate to ask them to design their own experiments. They still have the questions in their heads and they just aren't sure what they would need to do to answer those questions, so I gave them more specific suggestions about how to investigate these questions.

Some concepts, such as the conservation of mass, are not usually understood by children in elementary grades. Assessing them on their understanding of such concepts is both meaningless and unfair. David's knowledge of child development helped him decide which concepts to assess:

> Research has indicated that this is an age when some kids begin to see the conservation of mass when you change shape. I don't think it is that conclusive for this age, and because they are on a dividing line I didn't want to make that a goal of the unit. I want the teachers to be aware that some kids will say one thing and others will say another.

Kathy describes developmental considerations as they pertain to the assessments in *Earth Materials*, a FOSS unit for grades three and four:

> On the *Earth Materials* pictorial assessment students are given pictures of rocks—some dark and some light, some round and some sharp edged. Part of what we wanted students to do was look at the properties and make comparisons. . . . On the third question we ask for a Venn diagram. A lot of students can only look at one property at a time at this age, and you can see which of them have not made it to the next

stage of thinking. They would put dark rocks in one circle and sharp rocks in the second and rocks that were both in the center so that some rocks appear in two places. We tell teachers to use this assessment as an indication of the stage of students' thinking and not to mark them wrong if they can't do the Venn diagram correctly.

Assessment Placement

Before and after the unit: matched assessments

Pre- and postunit assessments are both useful, but only *matched* pre/post unit activities can document change over a specified time. Although curriculum developers for FOSS use matched pre/postunit assessments while they are developing their curriculums, the finished units do not contain matched pre/postassessments. The curriculum guides do suggest that teachers consider using preunit assessments before starting the unit. Kathy explains,

> We decided to leave it to the teachers to use the assessments for preunit assessing, and many don't. We did pre/postassessments when we were evaluating the modules and trying out the assessments to see if the students were learning what we hoped.

STC developers routinely incorporate two sets of matched pre/post unit assessments—a group discussion related to the central concepts of the unit and some additional activity, often carried out individually, to provide baseline data for each student. In *Organisms* students are asked to make individual drawings; in *Floating and Sinking*, students provide written explanations for a phenomenon demonstrated to the whole class.

To measure learning *related to the unit* the matched pre/postunit activities must reflect the experiences and learning goals of the curriculum itself. Keeping the overall goals in mind is crucial. David and Wendy say they have more difficulty designing these assessments than any others.

Discussions Matched assessments in many of the new science curriculums include a class discussion centered around a topic or question that is at the heart of the curriculum. Coming up with a question that is specific enough for children to relate to, is connected to the curriculum, is broad enough that everyone will have something to say, and can be naturally repeated at the unit's end is hard, as Wendy acknowledges:

> The preassessment has been the hardest part for me. This is probably the third time I'm changing my Lesson 1. I started out asking the children what they know about living things, never happy

with the information I got and not feeling I really captured the growth that I know that they had. So I reread my concept and learning goals, and I realized that my first assessment didn't really get at the heart of my unit.

During trial teaching, the preunit assessment question for *Floating and Sinking* ("Why do things float and sink?") elicited a lively discussion, possibly because students could relate the question to their experiences. As David puts it:

> "What makes things float and sink?" is the whole ball of wax. It's what the unit is all about. They talk about some of their ideas—what they think makes things sink or float—and that's a very rich experience, because the kids have a chance to say what they think. They re-examine those ideas at the end of the unit and it helps them realize that these experiences have taught them something.

David's last comment highlights an added benefit of matched assessments— student self-assessment. Since one goal of an assessment should be for everyone to learn from it, providing students with evidence of their own growth is important.

Tasks Finding performance tasks for pre/postunit assessments that are engaging, yield rich data about important ideas, and are nonthreatening is also a challenge. It is important to set out tasks that emphasize what students do know, have learned, and can do, rather than tasks that leave them feeling inadequate. A task can appear threatening both because of what is asked and because of the manner in which it is asked. The younger the children, the greater the limitations. Finding an appropriate task was especially difficult for Wendy:

> When I looked back at Lesson 1's preassessment, to "draw a living thing and tell me why it's living," I saw that it didn't measure what the unit was about at all. One focus of the unit is on living things and what living things need in order to grow and live. I'm going to have them draw a living thing and to include in the picture drawings of things that they think that living thing needs in order to live and be healthy. This will be the first thing they will do. I'll be able to do that again at the end and really have a measure of growth. It took me three tries to come up with what I think is a much better preunit assessment.

David used a demonstration for a preunit assessment. Like Wendy, he had difficulty coming up with an activity that was connected to the topic of his unit. In fact, the first demonstration he piloted was unrelated to the experiences within the unit and when it was repeated postunit showed no student growth at all!

> The preunit assessment I tried first, using bottle caps, turned out to be much too general and led off in all kinds of directions. It wasn't focused at all, and at the end of the unit when we did it again they didn't have any better sense of what had happened, since they hadn't had any other experiences with these bottle caps in the unit.

The assessment he finally settled on (see Figures 2–1a and 2–1b in Chapter 2) is tied to the experiences that occur within the unit and provides a better measure of growth.

Assessments within the unit

FOSS modules for grades K–2 include suggestions for observations, classroom discussions, and extensions that can all be used by teachers as embedded assessments.

The STC curriculum developers think about places to include assessments in several ways:

- They identify rich, engaging, juicy activities and experiences.
- They identify the natural wrap-up points for subthemes and subactivities.
- They look for those places where students are asked to apply knowledge and move a step forward in their thinking.

Teachers know what engaged children look like: absorbed, focused, excited, and conversing with one another. Wendy looked for such moments while teaching *Organisms* and then figured out ways to capture what students were saying and doing:

> When they had a particularly rich hands-on activity or discussion that I felt they would individually have something to spill out about, I designed an assessment for it. I was looking for experiences the children had that could immediately be followed up with a writing or drawing activity to get them to reflect on their experience. The children had a lot of dialogue going among themselves, so I immediately thought up an activity to get them to express themselves. Whenever I felt that they had a lot that they needed to say, I gave them vehicles for saying it. It didn't have to be written words—that's not the way that we get most information out of these young children.

A second way to determine where to place assessments is to start with the structure of the curriculum and identify natural break points, as David did in *Floating and Sinking*. He looked for transition points where activities shifted:

> I try to pick a couple of places in the unit that seem like natural places to look at what a student is doing or what they've produced, places where there is a natural transition occurring. In *Floating and Sinking* a transition occurs where students have been making predictions about whether things will float or sink. They begin to manipulate plasticene and suddenly take a step beyond passively observing what happens and are actively involved in constructing a boat. These transitions are good places because they are transitions in the kind of activity that is taking place and may or may not involve different concepts.

Another important transition in this curriculum occurs when students shift from investigating the *objects* that float to investigating the *liquids in which they float*, so David designed another assessment at this point. Other good places are points at which students are asked to apply something they have learned or to make conceptual jumps. The application of knowledge demonstrates how completely experiences have been assimilated and how accessible and "usable" they are. David says,

> In these transitions they are also doing something that involves more than what they were doing previously in the unit. They are being challenged to think about something that is more abstract than previous experiences were.

After several experiences making predictions about which objects float in *Floating and Sinking*, students begin to investigate bobbers, first pushing them under water with their hands and later pulling them under with a spring scale to measure resistance. David identified this as an important place for assessment:

> All of a sudden they are being asked to make a leap from sensing with their hands how well things float to using an instrument to measure quantitatively how well something floats. It involves drawing a graph, a major leap in a very short period of time. Now that leap either gets made or doesn't get made by kids, and it is a very important place for teachers to know what students are able to do.

In *Organisms*, students repeat an observation cycle four times, so Wendy included a written assessment activity each time. Repetition is particularly helpful for documenting progress with young children, because it allows them to become familiar with the format and concentrate on the content of the assessment. The repeated activity provides comparable sets of data. Wendy elaborates:

> They're setting up a freshwater tank and a terrarium, and there are two plants and two animals in each. Activity sheets ask the children to observe, draw, and describe each plant and animal. The students focus on a special characteristic and then record other characteristics they notice. The teacher looks for growth in their observation skills: Are they able to describe one or more characteristics of the organism? Do their words (written or verbal) match their drawings? Do they become more descriptive?

Postunit assessments

In preparing to develop postunit assessments, Kathy, Wendy, and David review the learning goals for their units to see which have been assessed and which should be assessed at the end of the unit, and then include a variety of postunit assessments—demonstrations, presentations, discussions, pencil-and-paper tasks, and hands-on explorations, as well as assessments for teams and individuals and student self-assessments.

Often what young children learn is primarily experiential and can best be determined by observing their investigations throughout the unit. Postunit assessment for young children can sometimes be confined to carrying out the second half of the pre/postunit matched assessment; there may be no need to determine what they learned in any other way. A drawing activity or a discussion is often sufficient postunit assessment for students in grade one. Wendy considered using a discussion:

> I thought I could ask the child to pick an animal and a plant from the terrarium or the aquarium and tell me a few ways they are like each other and a few ways they're different. Every child should be able to tell me one way they're alike and one way that they're different.

In the fourth grade, postunit assessments can be more extensive. The final assessment for *Floating and Sinking* consists of:

- The second halves of the two pre/postunit assessments (a discussion and a demonstration).
- A student self-assessment.
- A three-question paper-and-pencil test (e.g., one question is "Circle the hydrometer you think is floating in the water that is most salty").

- An activity in which students are asked to list as many ways as they can to make a mystery cylinder float.

When David develops curriculums, he likes to include paper-and-pencil tests to provide students with something tangible they can refer to and discuss with one another.

Following the format of all other FOSS modules, *Variables* includes three kinds of postunit assessments: hands-on, pictorial, and reflective. According to Kathy,

> With the hands-on assessment we want students to demonstrate their knowledge of content and their ability to *do* science (use equipment appropriately and follow procedures). With the pictorial we are looking at problem solving—can they *use* their knowledge and apply it to new situations? And with the reflective assessment we are looking at how well students express what they know and if that knowledge can be transferred to a new situation.

In designing the postunit assessments for *Variables*, Kathy and her colleagues at FOSS focused on the concept of using and manipulating variables as part of experimental design. Although one of Kathy's goals was to come up with assessments requiring students to apply their knowledge in a new way, she found this difficult:

> It is hard coming up with new ideas that measure the transfer of knowledge. For the *Variables* hands-on assessment we tried a number of things—rolling a ball down an inclined plane and varying the slope, and running a model railroad car down a track and varying the weight of the car—but they were too complex for classroom use. Assessments have to not only assess transfer, they have to be easy for teachers to use.

For the hands-on assessment, students first construct a pendulum and then try to determine which factors affect the swing (Figure 2–14a in Chapter 2 is a page from the assessment). Although they have tackled this problem in Lesson 1, the setup is different; for one thing, the string in Lesson 1 is replaced with paper clips on the posttest. Kathy found that some students see this as a whole new experiment:

> We began by changing the materials the pendulums were made of. We tried straws, fishing line, and other things. We needed something that would be easy to change the length of. Once we decided on paper clips we had to find the right size so that it would swing freely over a pencil. It seems almost silly, but that's the level of detail you have to be concerned with.

For the pictorial assessment, students are shown pictures of three experimental situations involving race cars, pendulums, and catapults and asked a number of questions about the variables affecting each situation. Two situations are investigated during the unit but the race car is new (Figure 2–14b is a page from this assessment).

The reflective assessment includes five questions: two ask students to critique experiments that are described, two call for definitions, and the last asks students how they could vary the accuracy of a pendulum clock (Figure 2–14c is a page from the assessment).

Criteria for Interpreting Student Work

All of the curriculum developers offer some criteria to help teachers interpret and evaluate students' written work and discussions. These criteria maintain the connection between instruction and assessment and enable teachers to track the same sets of behavior for all students. In FOSS' *Variables* they take the form of suggested answers; in the STC units they are guidelines.

The tasks involved in making up observation guidelines—pulling goals out of the unit, thinking about what to pay attention to while observing students, and possibly making up a checklist—resemble the tasks any teacher needs to complete in developing his own assessments. In drafting these guidelines for teachers, Wendy and David try to list important, describable behaviors. Wendy says,

> I want to give them some focal points, some things to look at when they're with the group, such as whether the children's talk is revolving around what they're seeing, if they're discussing things with each other, if they are working cooperatively, if they can describe orally what they're seeing and get it down on paper or if they can only do it orally, what they're focusing on—what's important to them—and whether they're questioning.

Assessment does not have to be something discrete that the student does; it can be the way in which a teacher systematically takes note of what is happening within a larger instructional framework. In *Organisms*, for example, Wendy relied on guided observation to assess attitudes:

> Assessing positive attitudes—this is where the observation log is very important to record observations of the students, individual conversation with the students, and behavior from the way they care for their plants in the cups to the way they hold their beetles.

Reviewing the Learning Goals

Wendy and David discuss where and how their learning goals are reflected in their final assessments. This step is both a summary of the assessments that have been written and a time to check whether they connect to the instructional objectives. About *Organisms*, Wendy says:

> The characteristics plants and animals share will best be assessed through the discussions and class charts of how plants and animals are alike and different, as well as the pre- and postdrawings of a living thing and what it needs to live. I will assess the idea that plants and animals grow and change through their seed books plus the discussion about their plants and animals and changes they've noticed. Assessing positive attitudes is where observation is very important, in addition to individual conversation with the students and watching behaviors such as the way they care for their plant and the way they hold the beetle. I assess their awareness of the great diversity of living things on the basis of class discussions, particularly when we talk about the diversity of life around school. This is a hard one, because it's something you have to look for throughout the unit. You really have to look for that in their dialogue.

Kathy checks to see if her assessments actually measure her goals by trying them out:

> How do you know if you are assessing what you set out to assess? Try them out with kids.

Advice About Developing Assessments

The actual activities curriculum developers carry out to develop assessments parallel the way teachers need to go about the task. Starting is the hardest part, and collaboration with and support from others is crucial. The developers you've met in this chapter have these suggestions:

- Find someone who is willing to work with you and talk with you, someone who has taught the unit or is planning to teach it. Two minds are better than one. David says,

> Talk to somebody else about [what to do and how to do it] because it's not something you can do in isolation—you really need to hear other people's ideas, maybe from someone who has taught those activities before. Find out what pieces of information you can glean and the most productive way to do it.

Kathy also brings up isolation:

The hardest part is the isolation of the classroom and only being able to try out an assessment once in a given year. Several teachers at one grade level might work together to develop assessments and then try things out and put their heads together. But teachers need district support to work together.

- Assume that your assessments will have several iterations. Try them out and then revise them. Curriculum developers frequently field test several versions of an assessment before settling on a final one, but even the final one may be changed. Just as you modify a science unit each time you teach it, you will probably need to change the assessments as well. David recommends,

    Go in there with a colleague and say, Okay—did this work? Did it tell us what we thought it was going to tell us? And how will we change what we do?

Kathy adds:

Be honest about what worked and what didn't. When it doesn't work, go back and look at what you were asking students and ask, Am I making too big a leap here?

- Make sure your assessments are balanced and not too long. Kathy has sensible advice:

    In thinking about your collection of assessments, balance process and content. Process is just as important as the content. Have kids do those processes as well as recall facts and keep assessments short. You can learn a lot without having long tests that kids hate.

- Look at the activities in the unit to see which can double as assessments. Kathy's practical, no-nonsense summary is an excellent way to end this chapter:

    You don't have to reinvent the wheel. First figure out what it is you want kids to get out of the unit. Then go back and look at the activities you have been doing and the extensions and focus on one of those as an assessment.

FIVE

Interpreting Children's Work

Everything students do reveals something about who they are, what they know, what they have experienced, how they feel, and how they think. Assessments based on ongoing work often elicit responses from students that reflect what is going on in their minds. Student drawings, notebooks, and graphs, however, need to be interpreted. How do we evaluate what we are seeing in student work? How do we identify evidence of learning? In language arts assessment teachers have learned to read student essays both for content and for how students make meaning out of text. Similarly, teachers need to interpret the products of students' science work.

One approach to interpreting student work is to set specific criteria in advance and then search for evidence of whether or not students have met these criteria. Do they measure accurately? Are they able to apply a specific test? Have they acquired particular knowledge? This approach is discussed in other chapters, particularly Chapters 2 and 6.

A second approach is to examine student work in order to discover how an individual student thinks, what he has learned, what she feels, or to use it for diagnostic purposes without predetermined criteria. This second approach can be of great value to teachers both for planning instruction and for understanding students better. Teachers across the country, in study groups and inservice programs, have discovered the benefits of interpreting student work with their colleagues. Although many of these groups have concentrated on language and visual arts, few have explored children's work in science.

This chapter focuses on interpretation as a means of understanding our science students better. With the exception of the first example, the children's work in this chapter is discussed from an outsider's perspective, without benefit of the insights the child's own teacher might have. As outsiders we do not know these children, their classroom settings, the directions they have been given, or the science activities in which they have engaged. In contrast, the classroom teacher knows both the child and the full context of the activity and can therefore supplement interpretations with additional information, providing a deeper and richer understanding of the child's thinking. Nevertheless, it is possible to come to some general conclusions about what children understand based on their writing, drawings, and worksheets.

When looking for evidence of science knowledge, skills, and attitudes, concentrate on the content of the work; don't be distracted by academic skills such as spelling, handwriting, or the ability to render a representation. Care taken in drawing, writing, and discussion is evidence of a student's investment in his work and his attitudes toward science and should be recognized, but the primary focus for science assessment is the thinking about science that went into the work. Feelings are also an important part of science, but they should not interfere with accurate observations. An observation is not necessarily "more scientific" when feeling is absent, but a description of feelings is not a substitute for a description of the content of an observation; it is an additional component.

Drawings

Second-grade physical science

Figure 5–1 is a series of drawings Lin did following his investigations in *Balancing and Weighing*, an STC unit for second grade in which students use equal arm balances to compare objects. Before making these drawings Lin had been exploring the comparative weights of blocks, Ping-Pong balls, and spoons. Figure 5–1 is a clear record of what Lin did and understood. His teacher commented:

> This was drawn by a student who spoke no English but was able to observe others to get an idea of the activities. I was never sure what he was gaining from an activity until I saw his drawings at the end of the lesson. He clearly grasped the ideas! These drawings show the objects he compared and the results he observed. Pictures 3 and 4 illustrate that he discovered that even when the block was turned different ways it was still heavier than the Ping-Pong ball.

Sixth-grade ecology

During a sixth-grade unit on ecosystems, students made and observed an ecocolumn (two connected soda bottles, a terrarium on top and an

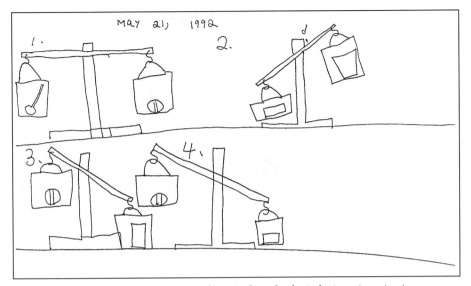

Figure 5-1 *Lin's drawings documenting his second-grade physical science investigation.*

aquarium at the bottom) in their classroom. Over several weeks, they recorded their observations with drawings and writing. Figure 5–2 is a drawing made by Kianga. Several experienced teachers studied Kianga's picture for evidence of her learning and made the following observations:

- She has some understanding of the natural sequence of things. There are bones of dead guppies and mold is growing on a dead cricket.

- She has a sense of scale that goes beyond her drawing ability. Objects are drawn in reasonable relationship to one another.

- She observed things in considerable detail. The guppy has gills, stripes, and fins in different places. The isopod has little hairs on it. One elodea has been stripped of leaves, perhaps by the snails. The grass has veins. These are drawings of actual objects: the organisms are not stereotypic, they are individualized.

- Organisms are where they are naturally likely to be found——the snail on the side of the column, the fish swimming in the water, the isopod on a blade of grass.

- The care she took with this drawing may indicate positive and involved feelings she has about her ecocolumn.

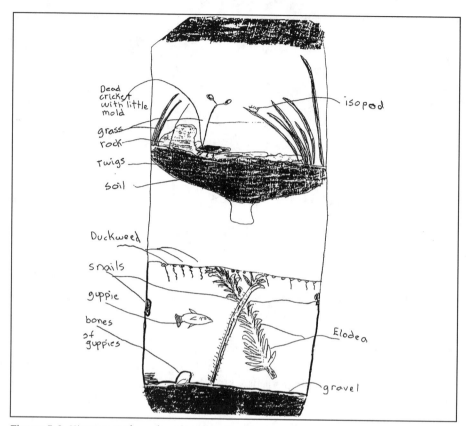

Figure 5-2 *Kianga's sixth-grade ecology drawing of an ecocolumn.*

First-grade aquarium

Eric's first-grade class set up and observed an aquarium stocked with guppies, tadpoles, and ramhorn snails. In Figure 5–3, he both draws and writes about a tadpole. Eric's observation provides us with clear evidence that he has actually observed the tadpole, as does his picture—there is a tadpole with two legs floating at the top of a tank of water. He also comments on its small size. The balloon words coming from the figure in the illustration may signal the importance of this event to Eric, especially since the tadpole's death is mentioned again at the end.

A stated goal of this unit is for children to develop sensitivity to living things. Eric's appropriate feelings about the death of a classroom animal indicate that he has such feelings; however, we do *not* know if they developed over the course of the unit or year. In any event, his observa-

Figure 5-3 *Eric's observations about a tadpole: "The tadpole died. It did grow legs. It was small. We were sad. Tristan saw it die."*

tion expresses feelings about science and about the world, and these feelings do not compromise the science; nothing is romanticized or anthropomorphized in this selection.

The references to Tristan, who witnessed the tadpole's death, and the plural "we" suggest that Eric may see himself as part of his classroom community (of scientists?); he is aware of other observers and of their feelings.

Written Work

The science work of students more accomplished at writing may include written assessments, structured written observations, and journal entries. The following samples of written work illustrate the evidence of learning and thinking they contain.

Fourth-grade chemistry pre/postunit assessment

Before beginning the STC fourth-grade unit *Chemical Tests*, students write down what they know about chemicals; at the unit's end they again record what they know. In the two-month period between the following entries Moira had extensive experience applying chemical tests to a variety of substances:

> What I Know About Chemicals
>
> [April:] I know some tur[n] coler. some chemical fiss and dissolve and [are] cloudy and clean. some look like glue. some chemical are good and some Bad.
>
> Questions I Have: Why don't it boup [blow up]?
>
> [June:] I know chemacals can dissolve, turn colors and fiss or bubble. A lot of chemcals dissolve. I know chemacal can be acid, Base or Neutral. Sum can be a Solution or Suspension. They can be a cristal.
>
> Satfy rules: Do not taste, wear your satfy goggles, follow Directions.

From the preunit writing in April we can tell that Moira has already had some experience with chemicals. Perhaps she studied another unit on chemicals, perhaps she or a friend owns a chemistry set, or perhaps she has been around adults carrying out investigations. Whatever her experience, we can see that she is coming to this curriculum unit with prior knowledge about chemicals. Her comments are specific: chemicals fizz, they dissolve, they turn color. She knows that chemicals change state. Her final question, "Why don't it blow up?" suggests that she is either anxious about chemicals or excited by the possibility that they can blow up.

Two months later Moira restates her earlier knowledge about chemicals but builds on and refines it. There are indications that she has been exposed to new experiences; she has additional information about the three categories (acid, base, and neutral) in addition to knowing the words *solution*, *suspension*, and *crystal*. From this assessment alone we are not sure if her knowledge extends past definitions: would she recognize a suspension? Does she know how to test for an acid? Our uncertainty about the extent of her knowledge underlines the importance of combining this kind of end-of-unit test with a performance assessment in which students actually apply what they know. (At the end of this unit, for example, students apply the chemical tests they have used to analyze the contents of a marshmallow.)

But Moira has not just listed a series of words, she has clustered them conceptually. It is likely that she knows that acid, base, and neutral are exclusionary, related properties and that solution and suspension go together. These linguistic clusters suggest some basic understanding of the concepts.

Moira's interest in the dangerous possibilities of chemicals has come up again after two months. Her inclusion of the safety rules in her postunit writing suggests that she is more concerned with safety than with the pleasures associated with explosions. It is also interesting that she has placed this topic at the end of both essays. Perhaps she recorded the information being asked for first, and expressed her feelings and concerns second.

Sixth-grade notebook entries on ecology

The way observations are written up can indicate whether or not the students actually carried out the observations, how closely they observed, and their interest in the activity. In addition, observations may contain hypotheses, estimations, and predictions, all of which are useful for assessment.

The following notebook entry by Seth, a sixth grader, illustrates how detailed, specific, and quantitative observations can be:

> *Terrarium Observation*
>
> Eleven of the twenty alfalfa seeds have sprouted. About twenty-one of the twenty-six mustard seeds have sprouted. Sixteen of the twenty grass seeds have sprouted. One alfalfa seed sprouted in the grass section. There are little brownish-black seed things on some of the mustard plants. There are ugly little flower buds on some of the alfalfa plants. There is a strange min-[eral] that looks like copper in the soil.

Seth either remembered or had recorded the number of seeds he planted and has compared that number with the number that sprouted to get a propagation rate. We can tell that he planted his seeds carefully, since only one seed came up in the wrong spot. And he is doing more than recording numbers here—he is closely observing the seedlings, noting changes ("brownish-black seed things," "ugly little flower buds"). Seth's reference to copper indicates some familiarity with other areas of science.

A second student, Mary, studying the same unit, also provides extensive evidence of knowledge in her observations (our comments are noted in italics):

Guppies: The female fish doesn't move around as much anymore but the male fish moves around just the same [*comparison, then to now and male to female*]. The fish have been eating the elodea [*observed? deduced?*]. The male is small and has a big tail. The female has a small tail and a big body. [*comparison, noting gender differences*]

Snails: The snails are always moving around [*has observed them over time*]. One of the snails had eggs [*careful observation*]. You can see through the eggs and they are attached to the elode plants [*detail, correct use of plant name*]. The snail shell has a spiral top and a half ovel for the rest of the shell [*very specific and descriptive*].

Elodea: There are all bits of elodea floating and most of the pieces are bit off [*deduction? seems to understand something has been eating the elodea*]. The top of the elodea is a darker green and the bottom in a light green [*comparison, closely observed*].

Duckweed: The duckweed is getting longer roots, some have brown around them [*distinguishes some roots from others; has noticed change over time*].

Mary has made careful observations. She notes changes in both plants and animals over time and has observed differences between members of the same species. For example, rather than generalizing about duckweed and reporting "The duckweed is brown," she says, "Some have brown around them." She has also used vocabulary correctly.

Sixth-grade biology structured observation sheets

On structured observation sheets, predetermined categories define and organize responses as well as indicate what is considered important. Such forms can be useful, especially when you want older students to communicate procedures, materials, hypotheses, and data in a particular order. Structured forms generally elicit less information from children, since the limited recording space restricts writing and the predetermined categories can restrict thinking. The response you get will also be less characteristic of a particular child, but it is still possible to learn about student thinking.

The structured recording sheet in Figure 5–4 is from a sixth-grade classroom. Ronald responded in his own voice, using expressive language: "The guppies swim fast and slow. Their tails move back and forth while they swim." We can tell that he has carefully observed the two organisms. We don't know why the guppy was not drawn, but the snail drawing is detailed and not stereotypic. To describe their sizes he has quantified his data and taken care to measure (or estimate?) both guppies. Although it is not immediately clear why the "both guppies are female" entry appears under the color

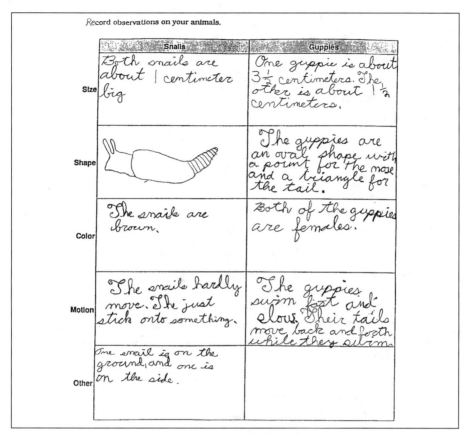

Figure 5-4 *Ronald's comments on a sixth-grade structured recording sheet.*

heading, it may be because coloration (in addition to size) differentiates the two sexes. It is also significant that he has appropriately and clearly organized his information under the different headings. We know that he is able to use this form to organize and communicate scientific information.

Sixth-grade physical science structured worksheets

Structured worksheets are often used when students are planning experiments and recording science activities. As part of a sixth-grade curriculum on time, students designed experiments to investigate the effects of different variables on a pendulum's swing. They completed a structured worksheet once they figured out an experimental plan. The worksheets in Figures 5–5 and 5–6 help teachers find out how well students can:

- Frame a hypothesis.
- Isolate a single variable.
- Define what will be constant.
- Describe procedures, such as the equipment needed, what will be measured and how.
- Make a prediction.

LESSON 9

Outlining the Team's Experiment   **Activity Sheet 3**

NAME: _____

DATE: _Oct 26, 92_____

1. The question (hypothesis) we will try to answer is: _How fast or slow_
   (is) the pendulum's going to go.

2. The one variable we will test is: _weight_

3. In order to make our experiment a fair test, we will keep all of these variables constant (unchanged):

   1) _starting angle_
   2) _size of washer_
   3) _length of string_
   4) _How hard you push_
   5) _____

4. Will we need special materials or equipment? _✓_ If so, we will need:
   cardboard, string, paper clips, washer.

5. What we will measure: _weight by adding more washers_

6. What we will count: _(seconds) how many times go_
   back and fourth

7. What we will observe: _"clock"._

8. What we think will happen to our hypothesis: _be like a real swing_
   peladrum and swing back and fourth (faster) slower.

Figure 5-5 *One version of a structured worksheet for planning an experiment.*

Experiment Planning Sheet

`LESSON`

Activity Sheet

NAME: _____

DATE: _Oct 26,92_____

Question we are trying to answer:

What do you think will happen to the frequency of the pendulum if you change weight

Variable we will test:

weight.

Things that must not change:

starting angle.

length of string.

size of washers.

hard push

How we will test:

We are going to test the weight by putting more washers on the clip and less washers on the clip.

Figure 5-6 *Another version of a structured worksheet for identifying variables.*

Graphs and Tables

Although less eloquent than words, tables and graphs are crucial vehicles for scientific communication and provide evidence of scientific understanding.

Sixth-grade physical science

Figures 5–7 and 5–8 were created by a student who completed the sixth-grade time unit discussed above. Stephen investigated how increasing

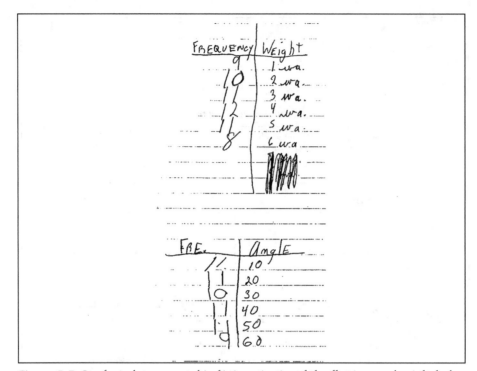

Figure 5-7 *Stephen's data generated in his investigation of the effect increased weight had on a pendulum's swing.*

the weight of a pendulum effected its swing. First he made a table of his data and then transferred it to a graph.

While his graph accurately represents his data, Stephen's data are not at all what one would expect a student to record for this experiment. The two variables do not maintain a consistent relationship; as the weight on the pendulum was increased the frequency of the swings first increased and then decreased. His teacher can see at a glance that something is wrong and can sit down with Stephen to go over the investigation.

Sixth-grade ecology

The table in Figure 5–9 was included toward the end of Jenny's science notebook for an ecology unit. Since many of this sixth grader's preceding

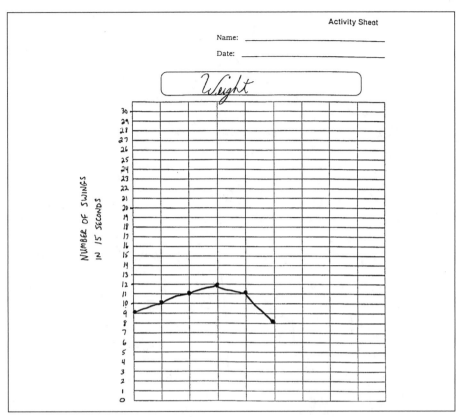

Figure 5-8 *Stephen's graph based on the tabular information in Figure 5-7.*

observations were incomplete and did not reliably indicate the extent of her work and thinking, her teacher may have been reassured to find this entry and be able to conclude that Jenny:

- Kept track of five categories of information.
- Could measure the pH, and had.
- Could communicate her data in a clear form.

The teacher might want to supplement this entry with a conversation to make sure Jenny understood what she had written (and did not, for example, copy the information from another student).

This is a summary of my observations of my ecocolumn over the past two mounths. Before I polluted the columns all my animals were alive. The grass grew. Then the animals died. They died because of polution. The fish died the cricet, pillbug and the grass died too. The animals died because of acidrain

Terrinm

Date of Observation	ph	# seeds	# animals alive	# seed grew
10-26	5.5	4		1
10-28	5.4	4	4	1
11-1	5.3	4	4	1
11-2	5.2	4	4	1
11-3	5.1	4	4	1
11-20	5.0	4	4	1
11-22	4.9	4	3	1
11-24	4.8	4	2	1
11-26	4.7	4	1	1
11-25	4.0	4	0	

Figure 5-9 *Jenny's table on the effects of pollution.*

Conversations

Many elementary school teachers, particularly kindergarten and first-grade teachers, begin a new unit of study with a conversation about the topic to discover what the class understands and believes. This allows them to base instruction on what their students know and are curious about while taking into account their conceptions about the world. On the following page, Rhoda Kanevsky, a teacher, introduces a discussion that occurred in her classroom:

I teach first grade in a small urban school that is racially and economically diverse. Throughout the year I have whole-class discussions about science, with everyone listening and taking turns around the circle. I use these discussions to discover children's ideas and interests, to hear what they have learned from their observations, and to give them opportunities to think through their ideas and learn from each other. I ask questions, but I don't correct or modify what they say.

Most of our work centers around the study of life cycles, particularly the monarch butterfly in the fall and silkworm moths in the spring. In May, when we were raising silkworms, Natalie commented in her science diary: "Butterflies are caterpillars that came out as girls. I liked them. The boy ones are moths. Mine is two centimeters long."

I called the whole class together and said that Natalie's entry puzzled me and that I wanted them to talk about it together to figure it out. The first few comments came in a rush, but I grabbed a pencil and wrote down what they were saying as fast as I could.

As the children tried to find some meaning in her statement, I realized how much they had learned from our study of butterflies and silkworm moths. I was impressed by the effort they put into their attempts to understand and validate one another's ideas. Although Natalie's theory contradicted what they already understood to be true about reproduction, and about butterflies and moths, they did not dismiss what she said.

We have reproduced the entire resulting discussion, along with our commentary on some things outsiders can learn from this discussion.

A student:
I don't get it. How could butterflies mate if they are only girls?

Another student:
How could moths mate if they are only boys?

Another student:
Maybe not all butterflies lay eggs.

Another student:
There are boy butterflies or how could they mate?

Jean:
Not all butterflies lay eggs.
Maybe some don't lay eggs. Maybe girl moths lay eggs. But there are boy moths too.

From these exchanges it is clear that the students have the idea that reproduction takes two sexes and that they are puzzled by Natalie's statement. The last two speakers suggest that some butterflies are male.

It is not immediately clear what Jean is thinking about. She seems to be drawing some kind of parallel between butterflies and moths.

Lucy:
If they were only girl butterflies and boy moths, then how could moths lay eggs and butterflies lay moths? The butterflies can't marry the moths.

Lucy knows that different species cannot reproduce together and is using that as an argument that there must be more than girl butterflies and boy moths.

Reika:
How can moths lay eggs? Silkworms turn into moths. The silkworm turns to moths that lay eggs. If butterflies don't . . . a lot do lay eggs. . . . a lot don't . . .

Reika knows something about the silkworm life cycle. She seems to be struggling with that piece of information and the butterfly discussion: she is not sure how to put together the "fact" that some butterflies do not lay eggs with this whole discussion of sex and reproduction.

Jameela:
How come boys [are] moths and girls [are] butterflies?

Sarah:
Moths don't have to lay babies, because some don't.

Leah:
How do butterflies mate?

Anna:
Maybe some of the butterflies lay eggs? My dad didn't have any babies.

Anna is making a connection between laying eggs and gender, since her father did not have babies.

Tommy:
The butterfly couldn't find the moth because the moths spend most of their time camouflaged against a tree and the butterfly won't even know they're there.

Here is more evidence to support the class idea that moths and butterflies cannot mate. Tommy knows something about camouflage as well as about butterfly coloration.

Joseph:
They couldn't find each other because butterflies fly in the day and moths fly at night sometimes, and silkworm moths don't fly.

Here is a second supporting argument; Joseph knows that some moths fly at night, and that silkworm moths do not fly at all.

Molly:
The boys have to have women. It takes a man and a woman.

Jamal:
A silkworm needs wings, antenna. Silkworm moths don't fly. If they were in a house they couldn't get out to find the butterfly.

Another argument why silkworm moths could not mate with butterflies.

Reika:

I'm not sure of what Natalie said before. It's like peacocks. Because the boys have all the colors and the girls don't. Is Natalie saying that since the butterflies have colors they're girls and moths have no color, then they're the boys? But not all.

Reika knows something about sex-linked coloration. She also returns to the diary entry and tries to clarify Natalie's thinking, drawing on what she knows about other animals to do so. She is thinking logically.

Teacher:

Reika is saying that Natalie is saying differences in color have to do with differences between boys and girls. What other animals are like that?

Joseph:

Downy woodpecker. Bright red head on boys.

More students have some knowledge of animal coloration.

Amy:

Ducks had colors, mallards.

As you can tell from the above transcript, classroom discussions demonstrate that there are areas of knowledge most children share, other areas of knowledge tentatively held, and information that only one or two children may have. In this particular classroom, the children are used to expressing themselves and to listening to each other. They draw on their scientific knowledge to support their arguments and test what they are hearing. The students raise many topics: gender-based coloration, camouflage, mating habits, cross-species mating, the mating habits of butterflies, whether moths can fly, and whether all moths and butterflies lay eggs. They make connections between different kinds of information to form theories. (For example: Since it takes a boy and girl to lay eggs, the boy and girl have to get together. But if butterflies fly during the day and moths at night, they won't be able to get together, so maybe moths and butterflies don't mate.) From this discussion, the teacher can identify issues the students are thinking about that might be pursued as they continue to study moths and butterflies. Some of the topics are amenable to empirical study as the children observe larvae metamorphosing into butterflies and silkworms going through their life cycle.

Science Journals

Analyzing an individual notebook entry or discussing a graph or chart provides insight into what students have accomplished at one particular point in a unit. It is the active assessment equivalent of a test. In contrast, a journal analyzed in its entirety can be a rich resource that provides information about how a child's thinking, skills, and attitudes have changed over time.

The value and quality of a journal depend not only on the science activities in the classroom but also on the student's writing experience, the value placed on writing in that classroom and that school system, the time allotted to writing, and how the journal is structured. The entries in fourth grader Anna's science journal, reproduced below, span September through January. The first and last entries can serve as a pre/postassessment, as discussed in Chapter 2. The journal taken as a whole offers additional information about this student.

9/8/90* I don't like science because I feel it's boring. I think it's a waste of time and would rather be spelling or writing a story. I would like to just skip it, because it's not interesting and it's boring. Not hard, or too easy, just plain boring. I also think that's how other people feel, or at least some of them.

9/11/90 Observing the microscope. First, the reader read the directions on how to use the microscope. Next, the gopher got the microscope and put it on his desk. We looked at its parts, then tried to draw it. The reporter wrote if we behaved, and we did. It was kinda fun, but I'd rather be reading, because it was boring but not as boring as writing in this journal.

9/13/90 We cut out e's to put on a slide. The researcher cut them out of newspaper and put the smallest one on a piece of glass. We covered the e and then looked at the others with a hand lens. After that we drew what we saw. Then we looked through the microscope. We drew what we saw again.

What is in the bag? I see different colored ovals, about 75 of them. You can eat these little ovals, and they tase delicious. They melt in your moth and the choclate tastes lusious. We sorted and graphed M&M's. There are 254 in the bag plus about 50 more.

9/18/90 When I looked through the microscope at an onion skin I thought it looked wet, kind of drops of water were on it. What I thought was water was actually

9/21/90 The onion skin in the [drawing] is scribbles and has lots of circles in it. The scribbles are wrinkles and the circles are cells. The hair has a dark line through it and light zig-zags in it.

---

*Entries that are out of chronological order appeared that way in the journal; Anna apparently occasionally inserted clarifying entries later.

10/22/90 The first thing we did, once we got our supplys, was lable the jars. Then we put pond water in the jars. In jar A we put six grains of rice. Then Ben saw two bugs and put them in the jars. We found out they were caddis fly larvas. Our half's jar (which was A) had microscopic bugs at the top, and we couldn't identify them. I couldn't see the rice anymore so either the larva ate it (or the little bugs did) or it's buried in the sand. I hope the caddis fly larva will turn into a caddis fly. I hope the same for the larva in jar B (Ben and Andrew's side), which didn't have any tiny bugs swimming around in it. [Here there is a drawing of larvae and of little bugs.]

9/25/90 In my pond water I saw a tiny beetle. It was so tiny I couldn't see it until we put it under the microscope with some pond water. It didn't move so I don't know if it was alive. It looked like an ordinary beetle, just in water.

9/26/90 We found a bug in our pond water, but we couldn't get it into focus, so we had to use dirt. When we mde our dirt slide, we got air bubbles in it. The bubbles look like circles on dark brown dirt. The cover slip was scratched, so we saw scratch marks.

10/1/90 The Watermelon Festival. When we estimated the weight and mass of the watermelon I guessed 7 pounds, 15 inches, and 47 centimeters. It was really 16 pounds and 3 quarters, 74 centimeters, and 30 inches. I was way off.

10/18/90 An Apple. An apple is red, with some greenish parts. It is in a circular shape, but is sometimes bumpy. It has a little stem, and some bruises are visible. An apple can have a sweet or tart taste, and both are well-liked.

10/26/90 Yesterday we put little brown specks in our pond water jar B (no food). We also put the sand-like circles in a jar with salt water. Then we labeled it C. We later found out the brown specks were sea monkeys eggs. We will try to hatch them into sea monkeys. (If the caddis fly larva doesn't eat them.)

10/23/90 Today we observed any changes in our pond water. At first we thought our caddis fly larvas died, but they were just sleeping. The little bugs in jar A were alive, too.

10/24/90 We had to write a description about a green Cuisenaire rod. It was small, rectangular, smooth, and many other things. Then the reader from each group read their group's report on the rod.

11/6/90 After we checked to see if there was any changes in our pond water, we wrote them down. In jar A, algae was growing and our caddis fly larva is dead. I didn't know it had bones but it did. Jar B had more bugs in it, and, like jar A, little plants in it.

11/13/90 Our sea monkey jar (C) looks like ice. But what really happened was the salt in the water sucked up the water, but not all of it. Some sea monkey eggs got carried up by the water and stuck to the sides. None of them hatched. I think that's becuse they were too crowded and the water evaporated. We will see if they hatch next time.

11/16/90 Today the sea monkeys hatched. Well, most of them anyway. They look like little white dots with tails. They are all swimming around quickly, and we fed them some yeast.

11/21/90 Yesterday we looked at sea monkeys and their eggs under a microscope. The eggs were big and brown and roundish. The sea monkeys were clear with a bright orange stripe down the middle. (It's funny because orange is such a bright color and you can't see it even with a hand lens.) They moved in spurts, as if they were jerking forward, stopping for a split second, and jerking forward again. The sea monkey had six little legs, or fins (I couldn't tell which) and I think they use them to swim about, but they probably use their tails too.

1/29/91 Now I feel different about science than I did at the beginning of the year. Since there are no science books, or tests, I think science is more fun than last year (or second grade). The only things I don't like about science is I [am] sick of my science group (maybe we should change) and writing everything in the science journal. But, however, I like looking at things under the microscope and the aquarium. But a couple of fish have died, and I'm sad about that. I hope that no more die and we fix the tank. I think the tank was the problem.

Several entries express Anna's *attitudes*. From September to January, her attitude toward science shifted from finding it boring to finding it fun. Initial negative comments about writing in her journal stop. She says she does not like working with her group, although in her 10/22 comments she hopes that her teammates' larvae will also hatch. Anna is emotionally connected to what is going on in her science class; she cares whether her caddis fly larvae hatch or not, and feels sad when her fish die. It is worth noting that when her watermelon estimate was "way off" she did not appear to mind; sometimes students change predictions and estimates to be "right" after the fact. She, however, seems comfortable with her results.

Anna's science *skills* are revealed in various ways. Her scientific observations become increasingly long, and she offers hypotheses to explain events in the pondwater jars. She gradually includes more detail as she writes about the organisms. For example, in her 11/21 entry she observes, "They moved in spurts, as if they were jerking forward, stopping for a split second, and jerking forward again."

We know that she can use a microscope appropriately: she focused correctly on the onion skin or she would not have described the "scribbles" and "circles" (which she identified as cells). She and her partner also had a good approach (using water) for viewing the tiny beetle on 9/25. We also know she uses cover slips, and has handled a hand lens.

She and her group carefully set up and labeled jars and kept track of what was happening in each.

Other entries attest to her knowledge of both *facts* and *concepts*. She uses technical vocabulary and sets her observations within the framework of scientific theory.

A group of classroom teachers who read and discussed Anna's journal found much evidence of learning expressed there. They categorized the evidence among "attitudes," "science skills," "knowledge," and "other." They also concluded that these categories would be a useful framework for assessing other journals. Their categorized observations were:

- Attitudes:
  like/dislike science
  focus—more attention to task
  about writing (no change)
  excitement—"see if they hatch"
  about life/death
  working with others
  maturity (ambiguity, distance)

- Science Skills:
  observation
  hypothesis "I think" (fish tank)
  describes with numbers
  use of materials
  use of microscope
  hand lens
  estimation "way off"

- Knowledge:
  vocabulary—names, structures, functions
  onion skins
  theories—"suck up . . . evaporate"

- Other:
  record keeping
  representing data
  drawings

Lab Reports

As a final sample of student work that can provide evidence of learning, we present an eighth-grade lab report. A detailed lab report, like a journal, covers a period of time and may provide information about several aspects of a student's accomplishments in science. In Laura's report, which was accompanied by two illustrations not reproduced here, she was responding to questions posed by her teacher.

Materials List
1. Funnel
2. Water
3. Solid mixture
4. Test tubes
5. Stoppers
6. Filter paper
7. Evaporating dish
8. Burner
9. Burner stand screen

Procedures and Questions
1. Put about 1.5g of the mixture into a test tube
2. Add 5 cm^3 of water to the test tube
3. Stopper the test tube and shake for several minutes

Q. *Do you think that either solid dissolved?*

A. Yes, I do. I think that a solid dissolved because when we boiled off the clear liquid (which appeared to be only water), there was a crusty, white crystallized form of a solid left in the evaporating dish. I would guess that this solid quickly dissolved into the water, but it was clear, so that it was not until we had finished the exeperiment that we realized there had been another component besides water in the clear solution.

4. Filter out the undissolved material
5. Wash the precipitate left on the paper by pouring an additional 10 cm^3 of water into the funnel

Mr. Lawrence, we forget to do this step. However, you said that it would not influence the outcome so we did not re-do the experiment.

6. Put the clear liquid into an evaporating dish
7. Boil it to dryness

Q. *Have the two substances been separated?*

A. Yes, the two substances have been separated into a yellow solid and a white. The white solid is bubbly and a bit [like] hardened salt crystals, probably because of the heating, and the yellow solid is lumpy and sticks to the funnel, due to wetness.

The amount of detail in the report indicates that Laura actually carried out the work, and her answers to the teacher's questions demonstrate that she understands what occurs when one substance dissolves in another and when the two are separated again by a process of evaporation. The care with which the drawings are rendered and the report is written show that she is committed to the work and has made an effort.

Summarized Guidelines

Several guidelines may prove useful as you set out to reflect on and interpret student work. We want to emphasize that the task is immeasurably enriched when interpretations are shared with and augmented by your peers. In addition, each member of such a conversation acts as a check on the others, pointing out assumptions that have been made and conclusions that have been erroneously drawn from the work. Here are the guidelines:

- Sit down with the student work you have chosen to interpret and note what immediately strikes you about it, such as whether the work is extensive, sloppy, careful, interesting, unusual, humorous, or inaccurate.
- Look for the level of detail and specificity in descriptions and drawings.
- If you are examining an observational drawing, try to determine if it is schematic and stereotypic or appears to be drawn from an actual plant or animal. The lines on a true observational drawing may be less "straight," containing wiggles that correspond to the true organism.
- If appropriate, note whether the objects in the drawing are in realistic positions relative to each other (as the objects are in the ecocolumn on page 90, for example).
- Pay attention to how the student uses words: language can indicate underlying concepts, as discussed in relation to the chemistry assessment on page 92.
- If you are looking at a journal or notebook, compare earlier and later entries for what they can tell you about the student's growth or change in attitudes.
- Look for expressions of attitudes and feelings.

- Look for evidence that the student has acquired information (vocabulary, facts).
- Look for evidence of conceptual knowledge.
- Look for indications that the student has achieved skills in using equipment.
- Look for indications that the student has carried out scientific processes.

Remember that you are interpreting a specific student's thinking, feeling, and learning on the basis of few pieces of work. Even the best interpretations based on the evidence may not be completely accurate; check your interpretations and hunches by talking with your students, observing them, and collecting additional work for interpretation.

Scoring

♦

A small group of teachers meets weekly to discover what we can learn about the children's understanding of science from their drawings, notebooks, and constructions. Today, Ruth Roberts arrives quite excited, waving a child's drawing for all of us to see. Ruth teaches a special needs class. Her children have spent the last few weeks planting seeds and watching the plants grow. This drawing is by Bryan, a boy who hardly pays attention and seldom carries out assignments. When she asked the children to summarize what they had done, Bryan was indifferent as usual but, at the last minute, drew a picture. Ms. Roberts didn't expect much since Bryan's drawings are often unrelated to class activities. "Look at this drawing," Ruth says. "He's got it all here: the plants in their containers, how they grow, the watering can. This is the first evidence Bryan has provided me all year that he is engaged and learning something."

The Need for Scoring

Ruth was able to use Bryan's drawing to document learning because she had established criteria for what she wanted from her assessment: concrete evidence that the student had been engaged and had done the work. Bryan received a high score because he had met these criteria.

A major obstacle to adopting active assessment in science is concern about scoring. Recognizing that assessments must be amenable to scoring is essential if multiple-choice tests are to be seriously challenged in schools. Scoring, and its inevitable consequence—children will be judged and perhaps ranked—are inescapable facts of school life. Even those of us who advocate less competitive and more cooperative education, who feel strongly that all children can learn and that all need positive, encouraging, and supportive teaching, recognize that there are times when it is legitimate to describe a child's progress in relation to predetermined standards.

The possibility of scoring—placing assessments in some rank order—must be part of any assessment system. The following types of questions, frequently asked by parents and teachers, are usually answered by referring to some form of scoring:

1. Where is this child along a defined continuum? What evidence is there that she is making progress, and how much progress is she making?

2. Where is this child in comparison to some external standard for a specific age or grade? Is he within a normal range of progress? Does he meet established community or national criteria?

Fortunately, active assessments can answer these questions. Whether you use a single assessment, such as a notebook or a drawing, or a comprehensive system involving extensive collections of work, it is possible to convert the data into categories that permit scoring and allow evaluative statements to be made.

The Uses of Scoring

Assessment involves judgment. Converting assessments to scores facilitates making these judgments. In the classroom, teachers usually know more about their children than their test scores reveal and can moderate their judgments by using this additional information. In previous chapters, we demonstrated how active assessments allow teachers to make informed judgments. As we move away from the classroom to other audiences interested in assessment—administrators, public officials, and policy makers—willingness to look at detailed information decreases. The legislature, the school superintendent, or the State Department of Education staff may insist on receiving only "bottom line" information (i.e., scores and/or grades). Thus, a tension develops between teachers who know their children and policy makers who only look at depersonalized and decontextualized numbers.

There's no simple way around this tension. A school superintendent cannot look at each child's work, a policy maker cannot read many transcripts of classroom conversations. That limitation emphasizes the need for, and value of, scores based on detailed documentation of work. Because documentation can be converted into scores when required, the same assessment system can serve the needs of all levels. Teachers and children in the classroom can look at the results in detail, while the scores based on that work can provide valuable summary information to a school system or a state agency.

A scoring system derived from active assessments has the added advantage that it can be readily related back to what the children actually accomplished. When traditional tests are used, decisions about whether a child has demonstrated a thinking skill or the ability to use a concept must be extrapolated from an isolated score. The actual test questions may not even be available to the teacher or administrator required to make the judgment. In contrast, even reports abstracted from active assessments can be illustrated with samples of children's work to demonstrate the application of scoring criteria and explain their meaning. On the basis of national assessments carried out in 1990 and 1991, England's School Examinations and Assessment Council has published some splendid documents that discuss levels of science achievement as illustrated by children's work.

Traditional Scoring

The most common form of assessment in U.S. schools is the short-answer test, most often multiple-choice, that constrains the student to choose one correct answer from among a limited set of possibilities. A brief discussion of traditional scoring systems will explain why they are inadequate for assessing science education.

Pedagogic assumptions of traditional scoring

All assessments make assumptions about how people learn. Multiple-choice tests are so common that we sometimes forget they are based on a particular theory of learning inherent in the way they are scored. These tests, made up of unrelated questions that each contribute equally and independently to the final score, rest on two major assumptions:

1. Learning consists of independent bits of knowledge that can be randomly accessed and that are totally separate from one another.
2. All the questions are of equal value.

Both assumptions run counter to a growing body of empirical evidence about how learning occurs. The conception that learning is made up of isolated facts and discrete concepts that can be accessed independently of one another is no longer accepted by professional educators. This view is criticized even by many test makers, who are beginning to realize that tests constructed on this principle (largely to facilitate scoring) do not allow us to make adequate judgments about what students know and what they can do.

The concept that all questions are of equal value, whether they require a student to interpret a graph, remember a definition, or identify a relevant variable, is also open to question. For individual students, the different kinds of questions may pose very different challenges.

Some test makers claim that different types of questions probe different kinds of knowledge—some reputedly assess factual learning, others conceptual understanding; some probe for skills, others focus on attitudes. But we have no way of knowing whether this is true for any individual test taker. Since all the scoring is standardized, we can never know whether any answer (right or wrong) is the result of memory, chance, careful thought and reasoning, test-taking skills, peeking at a neighbor's paper, or some peculiar combination of correct and incorrect ideas that cancel one another out. Only by analyzing the questions and responses *with each test taker* could we find out why he or she chose a particular answer, and only then could we begin to understand reported scores and make judgments about the relative value of individual questions. That analytic task is precisely what the newer forms of assessment encourage.

The reputed strengths of traditional scoring

Reliability, efficiency, and lack of ambiguity are the three assets attributed to traditional tests. If a student completes a hundred-item multiple-choice test, the scorer has only to match the student's answers with the scoring guide and arrive at a numerical score. Although this score can be converted into a grade in a variety of ways, it can always be done relatively unambiguously. I can decide that all grades above 90 will be given an A, all grades from 80 to 89 will be given a B, and so on. Also, it doesn't matter who does the scoring; the score is determined by matching the student's work against a template and doesn't rely on *interpreting* the student's answer. Anyone with a key to the correct answers and the formula (whether simple or more complex) for converting the scores to grades will arrive at the same result.

Supporters of tradition argue that multiple-choice tests provide unambiguous grades in a highly reliable and efficient manner. This standard is usually held up as the one that nontraditional tests should match; if they cannot, they are of less value. However, it's important to note the price paid to achieve the three admirable attributes of standardized tests. Let's examine these supposed virtues in detail.

Efficiency There is value in simple, inexpensive scoring. The price of schooling, like everything else, is going up while support for schools is diminishing, so school systems need to economize as much as possible. Why give up traditional tests, with their easy, inexpensive scoring systems, just when the public is demanding that schools rein in their costs? But the complexity and cost of scoring alternative assessments is more than offset by the benefits derived from the process, as we saw in Chapter 5 when we examined the value of using children's products to understand more about children and about classrooms.

Reliability   Reliability is a specific, technical term meaning that when an activity is repeated—a test is graded more than once or taken more than once—the results are likely to be the same each time. They don't reflect the prejudices of individual scorers or the biases of particular teachers. While this claim is correct, the price for this reliability is that the tests are totally decontextualized. Questions do not consider students' background, previous knowledge, or science experiences. Furthermore, the tests are usually administered in a bare room, devoid of familiar clues and separate from student work that might serve as reminders of correct responses.

But our understanding of how people learn increasingly recognizes the importance of context. Neither ideas nor facts are learned in a vacuum, but are assimilated into existing intellectual and social frameworks. By asking for answers out of context, we generally underestimate what students know, in part because the emphasis on this decontextualized framework also limits the kind of questions we ask. Questions that are amenable to this approach tend to stress simple recall and abstract theory over problem solving and real-life situations. Therefore, the effort to eliminate possible biases associated with complex scoring systems introduces other biases in the limited kinds of questions we can ask; we have not eliminated the problem, only hidden it.

Lack of ambiguity   An additional argument in favor of traditional tests and the way they are scored is that the results are unambiguous. We "know" what a score of 90 out of 100 or a grade of B means. But although the score may be unambiguous, there is still unending debate about the *meaning* of test results. The top score possible on an SAT test, 800, means unambiguously that the student has scored three standard deviations above the mean, *not* that the student has achieved a perfect score! A grade equivalent of 5.5 on a second-grade reading test does *not* mean that the student reads like a typical fifth grader half way through the year. (No fifth grader may ever have taken the second grade reading test!) It is a designation given to a particular category of high scores, based on a formula that may have little empirical support.

The National Assessment of Educational Progress (NAEP), which calls itself "The Nation's Report Card," may report that about ten percent of students age thirteen can analyze scientific data and procedures. But what the test results actually show is that ten percent of the students who took the test gave the correct answers to multiple-choice questions that are assumed to assess these skills. The students neither gathered scientific data nor developed analysis procedures.

Most public statements about what students know (or don't know) based on standardized tests are an extrapolation from the actual results. Policy changes, such as adding a correction for random guesses or discounting a question that was determined to be discriminatory, may change scores on standardized tests. Grade inflation may change the formula for converting scores into grades. When the results from such tests are used to compare schools, teachers, or school systems, even further extrapolations are required. That contributes to the acrimonious and irresolvable debates about test results.

A General Outline for Scoring
Active Assessments

If we abandon traditional scoring systems, we need to build alternative ones. Nontraditional forms of assessment provide records of what has happened. These products—drawings, written material, objects, recorded conversations—must be interpreted to be of use. The criteria used to interpret them form the basis for scoring schemes. For example, in judging a student's graph of an experiment, you might note whether the axes have been labeled. In looking at a transplanted seedling, you might check the depth of planting, note whether the seedling is still alive, and look for evidence of an appropriate watering schedule. In looking at a drawing of a mealworm, you might verify that particular body parts are included and that they are rendered in the appropriate color.

All methods of converting the documentary evidence into a score involve three components:

1. The criteria used for evaluation need to be defined.
2. The levels of achievement of the criteria need to be described.
3. A rank order has to be assigned to the levels.

Whether or not to convert scores into grades requires additional judgments. It is a possible further step, but not necessary for a quantitative scoring system.

Developing criteria

In order to establish scoring systems, you have to decide what learning you value; what behaviors, skills, and products you plan to observe. This may seem like a massive task, but it is essential (and it is usually glossed over in more traditional test systems). Chapter 4 describes how some curriculum developers go about this task.

At the national level, criteria for the appropriate content of school science are still open to discussion. A national committee was convened in 1992 to develop standards for science education, and its reports are still in draft form. But during the past few years a number of curriculum development and research groups and some state departments of education have begun to develop surprisingly similar frameworks for school science. The framework in Figure 6–1, developed by the state of California, has been widely emulated.

School science content is usually broken down into three broad areas (see Figure 6–2), although the area being emphasized varies depending on the group developing the evaluative criteria.

These components of science do not exist in isolation from each other, of course, and teachers should never organize their instruction by components. In practice, there can be no separation of the processes and content of science. It's impossible to measure without measuring *something*; any science concept is inexorably connected both with the particulars that contribute to an understanding of that concept and the science processes that have resulted in its elucidation. But for the purposes of interpreting and scoring assessment data, categories are useful, even necessary.

For most of you, the national effort to develop criteria and standards for science education are less relevant than your need to develop specific criteria for scoring day-to-day science activities in your classrooms. No matter what the national goals for science education might be, you need to decide what you expect your children to learn and understand from the activities you introduce them to. An example of a way to describe science skills by defining a set of criteria is provided in Figure 6–3.

Determining levels of achievement

Once criteria are selected, each one must be described in some ranked form. It is important to remember that *there is no universally accepted, absolute standard for judging the science activities of children*. We simply don't have enough information and research evidence to know absolutely what is an "appropriate" or "outstanding" observation for a six-year-old, or what level of experimental

Table 1 **Matching Science Processes and Content with Children's Cognitive Development, Kindergarten Through Grade Twelve**

Grade level	Science processes	Descriptions of content	Principles/Examples
K-3	1. Observing 2. Communicating 3. Comparing 4. Ordering 5. Categorizing	Focuses on one-word descriptions, discreet ideas	**Static-organizational principles** • Sea water is salty. Water in most lakes and rivers is not salty (definition by class). • Flowers produce seeds that grow into new plants (definition by function). • Machines are devices that make some tasks easier (definition by function).
3-6	1-5 above, plus 6. Relating	Focuses on principles, generalizations, laws	**Active-relational, interactive principles** • A force is a push or pull (relational). • Poikilothermic (cold-blooded) animals have body temperatures that vary with surrounding temperatures (relational). • Heat changes water from liquid into gas (interactive).
6-9	1-6 above, plus 7. Inferring	Focuses on ideas that are not directly observable	**Explanatory-predictive, theoretical principles** • Matter is composed of tiny particles that are in constant motion. In many substances these are called molecules (inference). • The characteristics of mineral crystals are the result of the way their atoms are bonded together in geometric patterns (inference). • When male and female sex cells combine in sexual reproduction, equal numbers of chromosomes from each parent determine the characteristics, including the sex, of the offspring (prediction).
9-12	1-7 above, plus 8. Applying	Focuses on inventions and technology; concepts, generalizations, principles, laws rephrased to suggest use and application	**Usable-applicational principles** • Selective breeding of plants and animals with desirable characteristics results in offspring which display these characteristics more frequently (application). • Use of the oceans and ocean resources is a focus of international conflict as well as international cooperation (application). • The development and use of more efficient lighting sources—fluorescent instead of incandescent, for example—is one way of conserving energy (invention; use).

Figure 6–1 *The state of California's framework for introducing scientific thinking processes.**

design can be expected from a ten-year-old. The science education profession is still in the process of establishing these standards through the use of active assessments.

*Reprinted, by permission, from the *Science Framework for California Public Schools, Kindergarten Through Grade Twelve*, copyright 1990, California Department of Education. Copies of the publication are available for $8 each, plus sales tax for California residents, from the Bureau of Publications, California Department of Education, P.O. Box 271, Sacramento, CA 95812-0271.

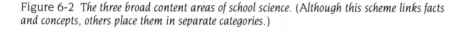

1. **Knowledge**
   facts (names, properties, definitions)
   concepts (general ideas, scientific "laws," overarching principles)

2. **Skills**
   physical skills (measurement, observation, manipulation, lab skills)
   mental skills (inference, prediction, planning investigations)

3. **Attitudes**
   toward science (care for living things, interest in science, curiosity)
   toward knowledge (questioning, risk taking)
   toward others (helping others, offering ideas)

Figure 6-2 *The three broad content areas of school science. (Although this scheme links facts and concepts, others place them in separate categories.)*

Developers of any active assessment scoring scheme need to decide what evidence would demonstrate full knowledge of a concept or complete mastery of a skill. The definition of levels for each criterion will be unique, and will take into account the local conditions under which children learn. However, in practice all the ranking schemes follow a very similar pattern. A generic scheme that can be applied broadly to all scoring systems is shown in Figure 6–4. A specific scoring scheme for assessing student products is provided in Figure 6–5.

In developing a ranking scheme, keep the following suggestions in mind:

1. Limit the levels. Too many levels of differentiation are confusing and impractical and make the individual scorer's task unnecessarily complex. Most schemes rely on three or four levels.

2. Relate your scheme to your specific situation. Any scheme needs to be tried out and refined in relation to what happens locally. Your system's definition of "can use standard measurement tools adequately" may be different from another's. Similarly, the ability to use measurement tools should mean different things when applied to six-year-olds than when applied to fifteen-year-olds; it will have different interpretations when applied to sixth-grade science than when applied to work in a spectroscopy laboratory.

3. Don't *over* define your criteria. Once a scheme is developed it usually proves manageable within its particular context, providing that the scorers have the opportunity to discuss it with one another and are allowed to make adjustments they feel are

	NOVICE	INTERMEDIATE	ADVANCED
Defining Questions and Hypotheses	doesn't form questions when encountering new information, ideas or experiences	draws on experiences to form focused clarification or inquiry questions	uses questions and knowledge to form several hypotheses; extends old or forms new questions based on findings
	forms variety of broad questions	can distinguish testable from non-testable questions; can refine testable questions	
Investigating	uses simple "watch & see" approach to investigating; can't plan beyond initial observation stage	plans what to control and compare but doesn't carry through in practice	uses preliminary or supplementary experiments to feed into main experiment; refines experimental design
	outlines general approach, but no detail on controlling variables	does experiments with treatment and control groups and replicates	
Observing/Monitoring/Measuring	sees only obvious things; no notice of details	defines indicators to look for/watch; uses measurements	can judge and carry out degree of frequency and accuracy of observations/measurements relative to needs/goals of experiment
	more active than passive observing; quality, accuracy inconsistent	able to follow regular program of observation and measurement	
Keeping/Transforming Records	sloppy, indecipherable or no records	accurate, but not kept regularly enough to see changes/trends	records transformed into appropriate graphs, charts, tables to clearly communicate results
	accurate records, but not comprehensive; sporadic, not systematic	accurate, comprehensive, systematic enough for purposes of experiment	
Collaborating	works in isolation; is passive to the detriment of group goals and personal enrichment	pulls own weight	effectively balances personal, group and task needs to maximize learning of all and quality of final product
	helps allocate work, set goals, make plans	builds on ideas and work of others	
Interpreting and Integrating Information	tenaciously holds original ideas; ignores evidence; doesn't integrate new information	bases explanations on evidence	changes/enriches prior ideas with new frameworks
	uses evidence selectively; jumps to conclusions by seeing only part of picture	able to interpret results from several replicates/sources; identifies trends	

Figure 6-3 A set of criteria for describing science skills. Source: Hogan, Kathleen. 1991. Eco-Inquiry: An Ecology Program for Grades 5 and 6. Millbrook, New York: Institute of Ecosystem Studies, p. 13.

Outstanding: All criteria are met, product or assessment goes beyond task and/or contains additional, unexpected, or outstanding features.

Good: Product or assessment completely or substantially meets the criteria.

Fair: Product or assessment meets some of the criteria and does not contain gross errors or crucial omissions.

Inadequate: Product does not contain significant number of criteria, does not accomplish what was asked, contains errors, or is of poor quality.

Poor: Student does not do the task, did not complete the assignment, or shows no comprehension of the activity.

Figure 6-4 *A general scoring rubric that can be applied to any scoring system.*

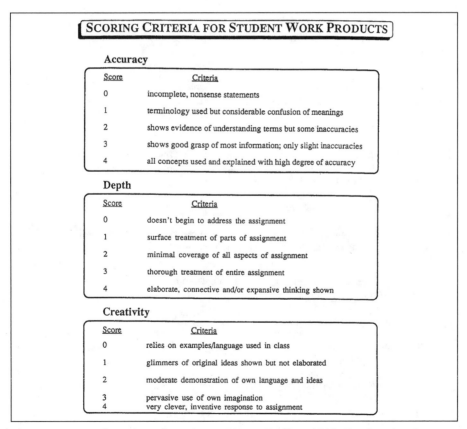

Figure 6-5 *A specific scoring scheme. Source: Hogan, Kathleen. 1991. Eco-Inquiry: An Ecology Program for Grades 5 and 6. Millbrook, New York: Institute of Ecosystem Studies, p. 19.*

appropriate. Don't worry about couching everything in strictly behavioral terms. Your scorers will be able to agree on the practical meaning of the terms once they have all looked at and discussed several assessments. One of the most comforting aspects of recent activities in science assessment is that many of the scoring schemes that have been developed do work and can be applied relatively unambiguously, with reasonable reliability, and can be described to others.

Most of the newer assessments in materials-based science programs do not provide scoring schemes. It is left to each teacher or district to develop them. Figure 6–6 is a sample scoring scheme for one of the final assessment tasks in the EDC unit *Growing Things*. It illustrates how

---

Question 1: Students are asked to measure the height of two seedlings, and record their results.

Scoring Rubric for Question 1

0 = No recording, *or* reports measurement that is off by more than some percentage determined by the teacher: for example, 50% of actual (i.e., two-inch plant reported as one inch or less or three inches or more).

1 = No recording, but reports approximate measurement. (The meaning of approximate needs to be determined by the teacher. Accuracy that can be expected depends on the markings on the ruler used and the children's experiences.)

2 = Records approximate measurement.

3 = Records accurate measurement. (The level of accuracy needs to be defined by the teacher based on the children's experience and the smallest markings on the ruler.)

Question 2: Students are asked to provide an explanation of their recorded measurement to their teacher.

Scoring Rubric for Question 2

0 = No explanation, or explanation makes no sense to teacher and is not related to any unit activity.

1 = Explanation relates to unit activities but does not explain this growth pattern.

2 = Single explanation given for this growth pattern.

3 = More than one reasonable explanation given.

Figure 6-6 *Sample scoring schemes for a plant unit performance assessment.*

carefully criteria need to be defined to be able to distinguish between different student responses, and how much they depend on the local application of the curriculum. The EDC unit gives a list of criteria for this assessment, but it does not specify details. For example, ability to measure is included, but there is no specification of what constitutes an acceptable measurement. This depends on two components:

1. The measuring tools available.
2. The children's experience in the classroom.

Whether a measurement is accurate or only approximate will depend on the markings on the ruler used. If the ruler is only graduated in inches, children cannot be expected to provide heights to fractions of an inch. In classrooms where measurement has been stressed and the children have had lots of experiences with rulers, it might be appropriate to add additional, higher categories to Question 1 reflecting repeated measurements, averaging measurements, etc. But *applying these added criteria would only be appropriate if children have had the opportunity to practice these skills during the course of the unit.*

Figure 6–7 is an actual scoring form from an ongoing research project on assessment at the University of California at Santa Barbara. It provides a means for scoring students' performance on an assessment of their ability to identify mixtures of "mystery powders." After learning to use simple chemical and physical tests to distinguish familiar substances, students are given a mixture of two substances and some of the materials they used in class and asked to identify the substances. The scoring form allows the observer/assessor to convert the record of a student's performance into a numerical score.

Assigning grades

Determining criteria and levels of accomplishment may be sufficient for many assessment purposes. However, if you need to assign grades, to make comparisons among students, or to compare individual students to a general standard, you will probably want to assign grades or numerical values to individual rankings.

The simplest solution for developing quantitative outcomes from qualitative data is to treat each criterion separately and to assume that each component of the score is equivalent to every other component. That way you can assign rankings to each level and then just add the scores. For example, if you are considering three criteria, each described by a four-level scale scored 0–3, as in Figure 6–8, then the three scores for

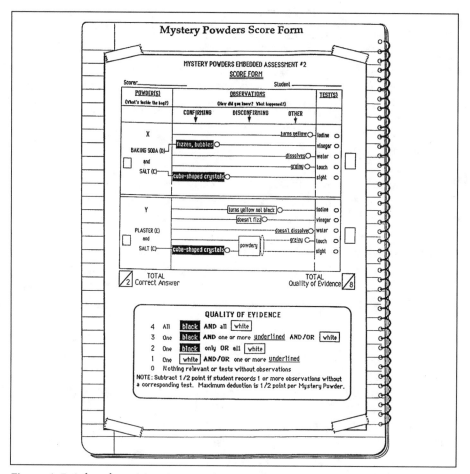

Figure 6–7 *A form for arriving at a numeric assessment score. Source:* Janet Harley Brown, Laboratory Notebook: Performance Assessment in Science (*Santa Barbara, CA: University of California, Santa Barbara, 1994*), *p. 36.*

each criterion can be added to arrive at a maximum possible score of 3 + 3 + 3 = 9. You should be aware, however, that while this approach has all the advantages and simplicity of scoring traditional tests, it also has all the disadvantages! Although the final score is unambiguous, it may hide most of the interesting information. If one of the criteria referred to knowledge and another to skills, then the final score by itself would not tell us anything about the student's relative performance on the two components.

More important, the actual assessment from which a score was derived may not have differentiated sharply between skill questions and

criterion	ranking	score	actual score
states problem	not at all	score 0	_____
	partial statement	score 1	_____
	essentially complete	score 2	_____
	outstanding	score 3	_____
formulates experiment	not at all	score 0	_____
	partial statement	score 1	_____
	essentially complete	score 2	_____
	outstanding	score 3	_____
carries out experiment	not at all	score 0	_____
	partial statement	score 1	_____
	essentially complete	score 2	_____
	outstanding	score 3	_____

Figure 6-8 *Sample scoring scheme, three criteria with four levels each, for an assessment that asks a student to plan an investigation.*

knowledge questions. The same notebook that was used to demonstrate a student's understanding of the theory of electric circuits was probably also used to demonstrate her skill at planning investigations; the same drawing that illustrated knowledge of plant parts may also demonstrate that the child actually dissected a twig. This use of the same assessment data for multiple purposes presents a variety of problems if the results are simply treated as independent additive components. Nevertheless, the assessment itself may still be more "authentic" than a multiple-choice test. The conversion of a student's notebook entries into a numerical score may involve theoretical and practical problems, but the classroom teacher, the student, and the parent still have the notebook, drawing, or product available as a record of work accomplished.

There are other ways of assigning numerical value to individual ranks and of aggregating data. There may be no advantage to coming up with a single "score" for science, nor may there be any need to do so. If different components are all considered of value, it may not be useful to combine all science components into one rank score. Language arts specialists recognize that reading is only one component of good language skills. Writing, the ability to use language orally, and reading comprehension are all components of a good language arts program. The distinction between reading and writing is now codified in many assessment programs. Similarly, we may wish to treat the different components of science achievement separately.

Atomistic and Holistic Scoring

The discussion above provides details for developing a systematic, explicit scoring scheme for active assessment that allows unambiguous assigning of numerical scores to documentary material. It can be described as an *atomistic scheme*, one that breaks down the notebook, drawing, or other evidence into component parts and assigns value to each. It is also possible to develop a *holistic scheme*, in which the scorer looks at the whole piece of work as a unit and decides on a grade or mark based on the extent to which the work meets a set of overall, general criteria.

Atomistic, analytic scoring

The major advantage of detailed analytic schemes for scoring is their clarity, to the benefit of both scorer and student. If the domains and levels of achievement are understood by all, there can be little question about a particular score. Such assessment schemes may be especially useful for diagnostic purposes, helping students improve their performance. The feedback to the student can provide detailed information about strengths and weaknesses. Some teachers develop analytic schemes in conjunction with their students, so the criteria are known before work is scored. On the other hand, developing an analytic scheme is time-consuming, and applying the scheme to students' work may slow down scoring: there may not be sufficient time to look at each piece of work in the detail required.

Some educators object to analytic scoring because it suggests that every piece of work can be analyzed for its separate components and that only the evidence of these components counts toward the score. The atomistic system does not validate the importance of a student's overall understanding and may fail to assess a student's ability to "do" science. Science is more than a collection of individual facts and skills. The only way to capture this totality is to develop a holistic scoring system.

Holistic scoring

Holistic scoring, an idea applied by all of us in making life judgments, was popularized and perfected as a scoring method by major test developers in response to the demands by writing teachers that actual writing be included in standardized assessments. The test makers learned that it was possible for scorers with a reasonable amount of training to agree on an overall grade for writing samples, and that an overall perception of the value of a piece of writing provided an acceptable measure of a student's writing ability.

The same kind of scoring has now been applied to science assessments. Holistic scoring relies on general criteria agreed on by the community using it and then applied to whole documents, such as notebooks, lab reports, or student products. The criteria should first be field-tested on sample documents and discussed among members of the community who plan to use the scores; when everyone agrees on the scores given to the samples, they will accept actual scores based on the criteria.

The advantages of holistic scoring are simplicity and speed. Another characteristic of holistic scoring, considered an advantage or a disadvantage depending on your point of view, is that it leaves considerable room for scorer judgment. If the person who does the grading knows the student, the grade he assigns can reflect the performance's relation to the anticipated achievement or other special considerations: Is this typical of the student's work? Was the student rushed in completing it? Did the student miss a group activity that would have contributed to the product?

Who Establishes Criteria?

Developing a scoring system closely related to instructional goals is best made the responsibility of the teachers who will use it. Doing so is a rich inservice experience; it makes you more aware of your expectations. Once you have gone through this exercise, you are also in a better position to defend your use of active assessments.

Nevertheless, students also benefit both from participating in setting criteria and from scoring themselves. In some classrooms teachers and children jointly develop scoring schemes, and each may assess the work. Figure 6–9 is a joint student/teacher evaluation using a form developed in a New Hampshire classroom. Figure 6–10 is an assessment scheme developed by a third-grade class in Maine to judge student presentations.

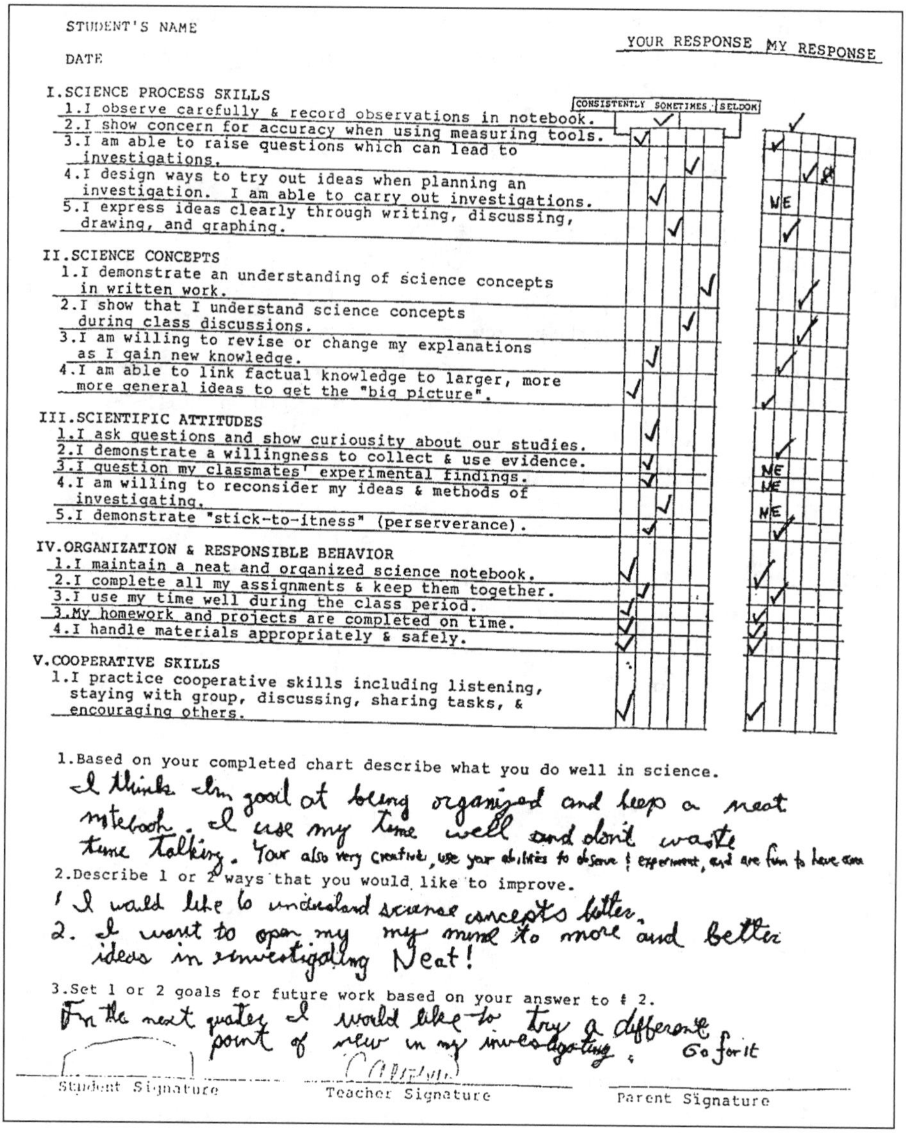

STUDENT'S NAME

DATE

YOUR RESPONSE MY RESPONSE

CONSISTENTLY SOMETIMES SELDOM

I. SCIENCE PROCESS SKILLS
1. I observe carefully & record observations in notebook.
2. I show concern for accuracy when using measuring tools.
3. I am able to raise questions which can lead to investigations.
4. I design ways to try out ideas when planning an investigation. I am able to carry out investigations.
5. I express ideas clearly through writing, discussing, drawing, and graphing.

II. SCIENCE CONCEPTS
1. I demonstrate an understanding of science concepts in written work.
2. I show that I understand science concepts during class discussions.
3. I am willing to revise or change my explanations as I gain new knowledge.
4. I am able to link factual knowledge to larger, more more general ideas to get the "big picture".

III. SCIENTIFIC ATTITUDES
1. I ask questions and show curiousity about our studies.
2. I demonstrate a willingness to collect & use evidence.
3. I question my classmates' experimental findings.
4. I am willing to reconsider my ideas & methods of investigating.
5. I demonstrate "stick-to-itness" (perserverance).

IV. ORGANIZATION & RESPONSIBLE BEHAVIOR
1. I maintain a neat and organized science notebook.
2. I complete all my assignments & keep them together.
3. I use my time well during the class period.
3. My homework and projects are completed on time.
4. I handle materials appropriately & safely.

V. COOPERATIVE SKILLS
1. I practice cooperative skills including listening, staying with group, discussing, sharing tasks, & encouraging others.

1. Based on your completed chart describe what you do well in science.
I think I'm good at being organized and keep a neat notebook. I use my time well and don't waste time talking. Your also very creative, use your abilities to observe & experiment, and are fun to have around

2. Describe 1 or 2 ways that you would like to improve.
1 I would like to understand science concepts better.
2. I want to open my my mind to more and better ideas in investigating Neat!

3. Set 1 or 2 goals for future work based on your answer to # 2.
For the next quarter I would like to try a difference point of view in my investigating. Go for it

Student Signature Teacher Signature Parent Signature

Figure 6-9 A *joint student/teacher evaluation form*.

Conclusion

Scoring systems can be developed for active assessments. In most school systems, scoring cannot be avoided if teachers and administrators are to

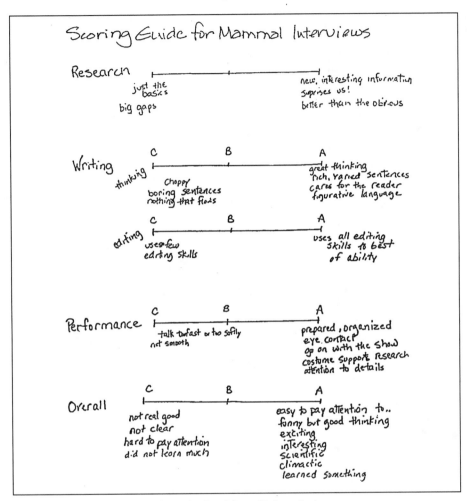

Figure 6-10 *An assessment scheme developed by a third-grade class.*

fulfill all the functions required of them by our society. Like other components of a hands-on, inquiry-based science program, this task takes time and effort and requires teachers and administrators to discuss what they value in education. But a scoring system for active assessments lets students know what is expected of them, helps teachers develop and improve their methods of instruction, and supports public understanding of a district's elementary science curriculum goals.

SEVEN

Assessment and Educational Values

◦ ◆ ◦

Introduction

Education is a political activity. Most of us are aware of highly visible controversies surrounding curriculum: whether to teach evolution or creationism, to provide sex education, to allow prayer in school. Other aspects of schooling—how children are valued, how schools are funded, and whom the schools should serve—are also discussed in political terms. They are debated at school board meetings, become components of political campaigns, and are subject to legislative or judicial action. Discussions about assessment are not usually addressed in this way; the issues are described in professional or technical language, as if divorced from the political arena. But assessment, no less than curriculum, involves our fundamental beliefs about how schools should operate. In this chapter we spell out the relationship between assessment and values in education. Anyone who decides to initiate active assessments should realize the broader implications of such an effort.

In the United States, assessment determines who is placed in special education classes, who goes to college, or who may enter high-status science and mathematics careers. It therefore cannot and should not be separated from other fundamental political debates about education. No matter what assessments we use, teachers and schools cannot avoid making judgments about children, reporting their progress to parents and the larger community, and taking responsibility for these judgments.

Unfortunately, no type of assessment can make this task either simple or without moral burden, nor can any type of assessment ensure that all children will succeed in school. Some children don't progress as fast or as far as others, some don't excel at particular subjects. It is the responsibility of sibility of teachers to acknowledge this—to gather the best possible evidence documenting the degree of progress for each child and to report it as accurately as possible.

Every assessment system expresses a set of values; none is neutral. Even so-called objective testing derives from a particular set of value statements. Some of these values and assumptions have been discussed in previous chapters. Teachers who adopt active science assessments make a political as well as an educational commitment. It is important to recognize the social, political, and moral issues involved, in order to become successful spokespersons for active assessments.

Assessment and National Education Goals

It has long been the hope in the United States that schools serve *all* children. Although our society has never achieved that ideal, the current educational reform effort reaffirms the American principle of equal schooling for all. The *National Education Goals* of the National Governors' Association reflect that commitment, addressing two issues that are particularly important if we want all children to benefit from education: that all children start school ready to learn, and that all American schools be free of drugs and violence, providing a safe environment for all. Most recent policy statements about school reform stress changes needed to ensure equal educational benefits for the entire population.

Various initiatives within the current reform movement call for specific improvements in the educational performance of our students. Each of these initiatives needs a set of criteria to determine whether the improvements are taking place. One call is for the United States to be first in the world in science and mathematics education by the year 2000. Such a claim requires assessment, since we can't have a rank order without a system for ranking.

A third component of current educational reform is the recognition of learning as an active process. This commitment to constructivist learning theory cuts across many different reform efforts. For example, many new national and state science curriculum documents do not prescribe a detailed curriculum to be learned grade by grade with traditional "scope and sequence" charts. Instead they provide "frameworks" or "standards" that contain general statements of principles and allow flexibility in what is taught and when it is to be learned.

Assessments Must Match the National Goals

Each aspect of educational reform has implications for assessment. Equity issues have raised concerns about the tests that are currently being used. The call for increased standards and improved performance is usually coupled with demands for more assessment. The new frameworks with their emphasis on the active learner also require new assessments.

Fair assessments

Assessments must be fair to all students. If a system discriminates against some students or some groups of students, then it does not serve all students well. This point is obvious, but how to bring fair assessment about is not.

In the past twenty years, politically diverse groups ranging from the National Association of School Boards to the parents of Follow Through students have complained about equity issues involved with testing. Examples that make the tests suspect abound: boys do much better on the SAT than girls and therefore receive a disproportionate number of merit scholarships (awarded on the basis of SAT scores), despite the fact that girls receive higher college grades than boys. Most traditional tests show a remarkable positive correlation between family income and test scores. Minority groups have repeatedly challenged tests as biased, and many of these challenges have been upheld in the courts.

The reason we need to worry about bias in assessment is not because tests reveal differences between individual test takers but because these individual differences on test scores are not randomly distributed in our population—they cluster among groups. Test performance by groups that are socialized differently is likely to differ. On various types of questions, girls traditionally score differently than boys, and on others, Hispanics, African Americans, or Caucasians are likely to score differently from one another. The causes of these group differences in test results stem from at least two sources.

Inequity in content The most obvious source of bias comes from questions or problems that favor one group over another. For example, some years ago, the Massachusetts state reading exams included a question that required the student to arrange in appropriate order a set of sentences that all referred to aspects of a baseball game ("Team A was ahead at the bottom of the eighth inning"). The item discriminated against anyone who did not know the rules of baseball, no matter how good his English language skills might be. Similarly, African Americans have proposed that IQ tests should include a larger proportion of questions whose content reflects the African American experience.

Items containing cultural biases lead different groups to respond to them more or less correctly. Clearly stereotypical language or prejudicial portrayal of some category of students has no place in assessment (or in education in general). Test makers now routinely screen questions for possible bias. This kind of assessment bias—either in unfair content or inappropriate language—can and should be eliminated. Most major groups involved in developing curriculum or assessment materials now have guidelines to help them prevent such occurrences. Figure 7–1 includes a useful list of equity criteria developed by the American Association for the Advancement of Science (AAAS) as a guide for reviewers for its monthly publication, *Science Books & Films*.

The shift to active assessments does not in itself eliminate this bias. Even though assessments are more closely aligned with curriculum or are embedded as part of the daily teaching activity, bias will still exist if the curriculum material discriminates among groups. Guidelines developed to minimize bias in testing also have to be applied to curriculum and to active assessments.

---

1. Where appropriate, does the material have equal male/female representation? Is the text gender neutral? In hands-on science books, are girls as well as boys pictured performing the experiments?
2. Are females and minority groups portrayed in a nonstereotypical fashion?
3. Do illustrations, photographs, or film footage include examples of minority group members, senior citizens, or people with disabilities?
4. Would the material be relevant in a wide number of settings (i.e., city, suburban, and rural) and to a wide spectrum of students (i.e., those who are economically disadvantaged)?
5. In hands-on science books, do the experiments suggested use materials that are accessible to economically disadvantaged students?
6. Would the materials be useful in a multicultural curriculum?
7. Are the materials free of religious bias?
8. Do the materials provide a balanced presentation of controversial (e.g., animal rights) or sensitive (e.g., AIDS) issues? Are dissenting opinions presented fairly?

Figure 7-1 *The AAAS's equity criteria for science book and film reviewers.*

Nevertheless, teachers who use active assessments do have an advantage in that they base their judgments on a child's actual work, not on a test score. The student notebook, the drawing, or the worksheet may inform the teacher of one child's or group of children's problems with a particular language usage, certain concepts, or cultural differences. When a teacher looks at actual work samples she is much more likely to recognize equity problems than when she grades short-answer tests. Active assessments permit children to demonstrate what they know in ways that are not possible on traditional tests. The illustrations in the previous chapters contain several such examples.

Inequity in structure Another form of bias is equally important, is more subtle, and cannot be removed by changing language or content. Every assessment method calls upon the student to use some form of thinking and acting from a wide range of possible thought and behavior. Asking students to draw favors those students who are comfortable with drawing, asking students to give oral reports favors those who are comfortable with oral presentations, and asking students to write favors the fluent writers. Asking students to fill in the little circles on a multiple-choice test favors those students who think linearly and exclusively.

Since it is impossible to assess learning without requiring students to exercise some skill, this second potential form of bias can be addressed only by extending assessments to include multiple forms of student response. The more widely you spread your assessment net, the more forms of assessment you use, the less likely you will be to favor any one category of students. This advice is simple common sense: teachers routinely modify their teaching style to accommodate the strengths of their pupils.

Using several different forms of assessment increases the opportunity for every child to demonstrate what she or he knows and provides the teacher with multiple opportunities to note cultural or racial differences that may affect his judgment of a child's performance.

Changes in assessment practices cannot solve all the problems of discrimination and prejudice in our society or the manifestations of those problems in American schools. It is not likely that changes in the way we assess children will alter persistent differences in student achievement between wealthier, suburban districts and impoverished urban schools. That gap cannot be eliminated without addressing larger social issues. But by adopting active assessments that require students to exercise multiple modes of thought and response, we can reduce the ways assessment reinforces biases in our society.

More assessments

Most calls for goals to raise standards or to improve performance also strongly urge some form of increased assessment, often assumed to be more of the current traditional tests. Advocates of active assessment must realize that simply criticizing the effectiveness of these tests is not enough. The push for increased standards is essentially neutral about the kinds of assessment instruments employed.

But the assessments used will certainly determine what is taught. To bring about change in testing procedures, we need to support the calls for assessment and ask whether a proposed test measures what is valued. Will the test tell us that our students have more of the skills needed in the work place? Will the test inform us of our students' increased ability to do science, or of their increased ability to take tests?

Appropriate assessments

Active assessment reflects the kind of schooling usually advocated in a democratic society, one that values each student and that is designed to facilitate success rather than document failure. The values of a school system are illuminated by the forms of assessment used. One criticism leveled against traditional testing is that it reduces the person being tested to a cipher, a passive test taker, who contributes only disconnected answers.

Positive emphasis Active assessments value individuals and are designed to bring out the strengths of students rather than to show up their weaknesses. Traditional tests leave students with images of questions they got wrong and things they didn't know. In contrast, drawings, notebooks, and other student products used for assessment often leave memories of things achieved and proudly accomplished. Individual students feel empowered and validated through their participation in assessments that provide room for individual (or group) projects, personal stories, drawings, and statements.

Reflective of educational values The active assessments described in this book contain messages to schools about the kind of teaching and learning that is valued. Advocates of democratic education envision schools as places where children make meaning out of their experience and are active participants in their education, not passive respondents to a set curriculum. Assessments appropriate to this approach require students to demonstrate their knowledge through action. Assessments have the power to influence curriculum and instruction. When New

York State introduced performance assessments as part of their elementary science program evaluation, the materials for the test—balances, thermometers, etc.—were left in the schools from one year to the next. In response to criticism that this might lead teachers to teach to the test—to acquaint their children with the actions required on the test—state department officials responded that they had no objection: these were skills they wanted all children to have.

Other agencies have also chosen forms of assessment that may influence curriculum to become more active. To quote the *Framework for* 1994 *National Assessment*, "by focusing on meaningful knowledge and skills, NAEP should be a force in fostering progress as well as measuring it, enabling more students to learn more science" (NAEP 1992, p.32).

Nonnormative reporting A striking and generally dehumanizing attribute of much traditional assessment is its basic assumption that student achievement can be described adequately by a normal distribution curve and that the midpoint of that curve represents "average" results. This assumption, for which studies of complex human activity provide little supporting evidence, is a prime component of many traditional assessments. Most national assessments don't even report actual student results, only scores that have been normalized to fit a theoretical curve. This leaves schools in the awkward position of being forced to inform exactly half the students that they are "below average." The efforts by school systems and state departments of education to avoid reporting low scores have been widely publicized. This burden does not fall equally on all schools. The approximately ten percent of the largest school districts serving a vast majority of our nation's children invariably end up with "below average" scores while the small but more numerous suburban systems generally tend to have "above average" scores. Since test results are closely related to socioeconomic status, this says less about schools and children than it does about the distribution of wealth in our society.

A striking characteristic of some of the new state-mandated assessment systems is that they do *not* report scores in the form of normal distributions. Instead they are developing ways to report student *achievement* based on some other standard of comparison. One form is to describe percentages of students who can accomplish something, have reached a certain level, or are performing as the agency would wish them to. This trend is reflected in the 1994 *Framework*, which specifically states:

> For the types of assessment exercises and assessment as a whole recommended in this Framework, the usual assumptions about independence of individual items and discrete properties of learners

randomly distributed throughout the population will not hold. For this reason, items, scales and students' test results should not be adjusted after scaling to fit a normal distribution curve. Instead scaling should be based on *a priori* definitions of scales. (p. 39)

Removing the normal-curve straightjacket allows assessments to be organized so that students' results can be described from multiple perspectives, and, most important, allows for the possibility that any fraction of students can succeed in an assessment.

Cooperative learning Recognizing that group processes themselves can be valuable for solving problems and helping children learn, many active assessments feature assessment of students in groups. These methods reflect current thinking about learning that has both a pedagogic and social basis. We value group work and cooperative learning in the classroom both because educational theory suggests that it is useful for learning and because we recognize that cooperating and learning with others have important social consequences for the ability of individuals in a multiethnic society to live and work together. By modifying assessments to reflect this value, we encourage and validate group work.

The Role of Teachers in Assessment

Many teachers are frustrated by their lack of involvement in traditional assessment systems: they teach and at some point their students take a standardized test, the results of which may or may not be returned either to the students or the teachers. In many cases the time lag between testing and reporting results is so great that the teacher no longer has the pupils when results are released. But even if the results are returned in a more timely manner, most teachers find the reported scores almost useless, since the results don't inform them about what to do next, how to modify curriculum to help individual students, or why some items proved to be hard for the students.

In contrast, the process of analysis inherent in active assessments, besides providing information about students, is itself rewarding for teachers.

Conclusion

Education is a real-world activity, engaged in by real students, teachers, and administrators in a complex, changing, and challenging world. There can be no perfect education in practice, and there is therefore no perfect assessment. Nor can assessments be free of values. All we can hope to do is continually to strive to achieve our educational goals, to learn from our failures, and to provide the best possible education for the children in our care. One part of this effort involves continually improving assessment.

Assessment is a particularly difficult topic, because when we assess children we not only demonstrate (to ourselves and the rest of the educational community) what children have learned, we also have to face our own limitations as teachers. Since tests can never be divorced from their context, the social conditions in which they are prepared and taken, our own work as teachers, and all the other issues surrounding education, we can only struggle to make our assessments consonant with our teaching, to use methods that allow our students to succeed, and to introduce the widest possible range of formats, thus maximizing the opportunity for all students to demonstrate their accomplishments.

Works Cited

Badger, Elizabeth, and Brenda Thomas. 1989. *On Their Own: Student Response to Open-ended Tests in Science*. Quincy, MA: Massachusetts Department of Education.

Badger, Elizabeth, Brenda Thomas, and E. McCormack. 1990. *Beyond Paper and Pencil*. Quincy, MA: Massachusetts Department of Education.

Brown, Janet Harley. 1994. *Laboratory Noteboook: Performance Assessment in Science*. Santa Barbara, CA: University of California at Santa Barbara.

Full Option Science System. Chicago, IL: Encyclopedia Britannica Educational Corporation. Units cited: *Earth Materials* and *Variables*.

Hoepfner, Ralph, et al. 1976. CSE *Elementary School Test Evaluations*. Los Angeles, CA: UCLA Center for the Study of Evaluation.

Hogan, Kathleen. 1991. *Eco-Inquiry: An Ecology Program for Grades 5 and 6*. Milibrook, NY: Institute for Ecosystem Studies.

Insights. Newton, MA: Education Development Center. Units cited: *Bones and Skeletons* and *Growing Things*.

McDermott, Lillian. 1984. Research on Conceptual Understanding in Mechanics. *Physics Today* V. 37 (July): 24–31.

Madaus, George F., et al. 1992. *The Influence of Testing on Teaching Math and Science in Grades 4–12, Executive Summary*. Boston, MA: Boston College (Center for the Study of Testing, Evaluation, and Educational Policy.)

National Assessment for Educational Progress. 1992. *Science Framework for the 1994 National Assessment of Educational Progress*. Washington, DC: National Assessment Governing Board, U.S. Department of Education.

National Commission on Excellence in Education. 1983. *A Nation at Risk*. Washington, DC: U.S. Government Printing Office.

National Committee on Educational Standards and Assessment. 1993. *National Science Education Standards: July '93 Progress Report*. Washington, DC: National Research Council.

National Governors' Association. 1990. *National Education Goals*. Washington, DC: National Governors' Association.

New York State Department of Education. n.d. *Guide to Program Evaluation K–4*. Albany, NY: State Department of Education.

Novak, Joseph D., and Bob Gowin. 1986. *Learning How to Learn*. London: Cambridge University Press.

Science Framework for California Public Schools, Kindergarten Through Grade Twelve. 1990. Sacramento, CA: California Department of Education.

Schools Examinations and Assessment Council. n. d. *Children's Work Assessed, Key Stage* 1. London: Schools Examinations and Assessment Council.

———. n. d. *Children's Work Assessed, Science, Key Stage* 3. London: Schools Examinations and Assessment Council.

Science and Technology for Children. Field test edition. Burlington, NC: Carolina Biological Supply Company. Units cited: *Balancing and Weighing, Butterflies, Chemical Tests, Ecosystems, Electric Circuits, Floating and Sinking, Food Chemistry, Magnets and Motors, Organisms,* and *Plant Growth and Development*.

Selected Bibliography

· ◆ ·

General Reviews of Active Assessment
(not limited to science)

Herman, Joan L., Pamela R. Aschbacher, and Lynn Winters. 1992. A *Practical Guide to Alternative Assessment*. Alexandria, VA: Association for Supervision and Curriculum Development.

Mitchell, Ruth. 1992. *Testing for Learning*. New York: The Free Press.

Perrone, Vito, ed. 1991. *Expanding Student Assessment*. Alexandria, VA: Association for Supervision and Curriculum Development.

Wiggins, Grant. 1993. *Assessing Student Performance: Exploring the Purpose and Limits of Testing*. San Francisco, CA: Jossey-Bass.

Wolf, Dennie, Janet Bixby, John Glenn III, and Howard Gardner. 1992. To Use Their Minds Well: Investigating New Forms of Student Assessment. *Review of Research in Education* 17: 31–74. Washington, DC: American Educational Research Association.

Active Science Assessment Research and Theory

Blomberg, Fran, Marion Epstein, Walter McDonald, and Ina Mullis. 1986. A *Pilot Study of Higher-Order Thinking Skills, Assessment Techniques in Science and Mathematics: Final Report*, Parts 1 and 2. Princeton, NJ: National Assessment of Educational Progress.

Hein, George E., ed. 1990. *The Assessment of Hands-On Elementary Science Programs*. Grand Forks, ND: North Dakota Study Group on Evaluation.

Hein, George E. 1991. Active Assessment for Active Science. In *Expanding Student Assessment*, edited by Vito Perrone. Alexandria, VA: Association for Supervision and Curriculum Development.

Kulm, Gerald, and Shirley Malcolm, eds. 1991. *Science Assessment in the Service of Reform*. Washington, DC: American Association for the Advancement of Science.

McDermott, Lillian. 1984. Research on Conceptual Understanding in Mechanics. *Physics Today* V. 37 (July): 24–31.

Miller, Robin, and Rosalind Driver. 1987. Beyond Processes. *Studies in Science Education* 14:33–62.

National Assessment for Educational Progress. 1987. *Learning by Doing.* Princeton, NJ: Educational Testing Service.

Shavelson, Richard J., and Gail P. Baxter. 1992. What We've Learned About Assessing Hands-on Science. *Educational Leadership* 49(8):20–25.

Shavelson, Richard J., Gail P. Baxter, and Jerome Pine. 1992. Performance Assessments: Political Rhetoric and Measurement Reality. *Educational Researcher* 21(4):22–27.

Examples of Practice

Bryce, T. G. K., et al. 1988. *Techniques for Assessing Process Skills in Practical Science.* Oxford, UK: Heinemann.

Carlson, Sybil B. 1987. *Creative Classroom Testing.* Princeton, NJ: Educational Testing Service.

Cavendish, Susan, Maurice Galton, Linda Hargreaves, and Wynne Harlen. 1990. *Assessing Science in the Primary Classroom: Observing Activities.* London: Chapman.

Doris, Ellen. 1991. *Doing What Scientists Do: Children Learn to Investigate Their World.* Portsmouth, NH: Heinemann.

Hein, George E. 1987. The Right Test for Hands-on Science. *Science and Children* V. 25 (October):8–12.

Hogan, Kathleen. 1991. *Eco-Inquiry: An Ecology Program for Grades 5 and 6.* Millbrook, NY: Institute of Ecosystem Studies.

Lipowich, Shelly, ed. 1989. *Designing District Evaluation Instruments for Math and Science Process Skills.* Annual newsletter. ASCD Network, 6321 N. Cañón del Pájaro, Tucson, AZ 85715.

Russell, Terry, and Wynne Harlen. 1990. *Assessing Science in the Primary Classroom: Practical Tasks.* London: Chapman.

Schilling, Mike, Linda Hargreaves, and Wynne Harlen. 1990. *Assessing Science in the Primary Classroom: Written Tasks.* London: Chapman.

Policy Statements on Testing and Critiques of Traditional Tests

Hoepfner, Ralph, et al. 1976. CSE *Elementary School Test Evaluations.* Los Angeles, CA: UCLA Center for the Study of Evaluation.

Madaus, George F., et al. 1992. *The Influence of Testing on Teaching Math and Science in Grades 4–12, Executive Summary.* Boston, MA: Boston College. Center for the Study of Testing, Evaluation, and Educational Policy.

National Assessment for Educational Progress. 1992. *Science Framework for the 1994 National Assessment of Educational Progress.* Washington, DC: National Assessment Governing Board, U.S. Department of Education.

National Committee on Educational Standards and Assessment. 1993. *National Science Education Standards: July '93 Progress Report.* Washington, DC: National Research Council.

Raizen, Senta A., et al. 1989. *Assessment in Elementary School Education.* Washington, DC: The National Center for Improving Science Education.

———. 1990. *Assessment in Science Education: The Middle Years.* Washington, DC: The National Center for Improving Science Education.

Standardized Tests and Our Children: A Guide to Testing Reform. Cambridge, MA: FairTest (342 Broadway, Cambridge, MA 02139).

State, Provincial, and National Assessments

Badger, Elizabeth, and Brenda Thomas. 1989. *On Their Own: Student Response to Open-ended Tests in Science.* Quincy, MA: Massachusetts Department of Education.

Badger, Elizabeth, Brenda Thomas, and E. McCormack. 1990. *Beyond Paper and Pencil.* Quincy, MA: Massachusetts Department of Education.

Baron, Joan. 1990. What We Have Learned from State Assessments of Elementary School Science. In *The Assessment of Hands-On Elementary Science Programs,* edited by George E. Hein. Grand Forks, ND: North Dakota Study Group on Evaluation.

Bateson, David, Gaalen Erickson, P. James Gaskell, and Marvin Wideen. 1991. *British Columbia Assessment of Science Provincial Report.* Vancouver, BC: Ministry of Education.

Mullis, Ina V. S., and Lynn B. Jenkins. 1988. *The Science Report Card: Elements of Risk and Recovery.* Princeton, NJ: Educational Testing Service.

New York State Department of Education. n.d. *Guide to Program Evaluation K–4.* Albany, NY: State Department of Education.

Science Framework for California Public Schools, Kindergarten Through Grade Twelve. 1990. Sacramento, CA: California Department of Education.

The British Experience

Assessment of Performance Unit. 1983–88. *Science for Teachers.* Nos. 1–11. A series of booklets based on the work of the APU. London: Department of Education and Science, H.M.P.O.

Evaluation and Monitoring Unit. n.d. *Assessment Matters.* Nos. 1–6. A series of booklets based on the work of the Assessment of Performance Unit. London: School Examinations and Assessment Council.

Johnson, Sandra. 1989. *National Assessment: The APU Science Approach.* London: Department of Education and Science, H. M. P. O.

School Examinations and Assessment Council. n.d. *Children's Work Assessed, Key Stage* 1. London: School Examinations and Assessment Council.

School Examinations and Assessment Council. n.d. *Children's Work Assessed, Science, Key Stage* 3. London: School Examinations and Assessment Council.

Publications in this last section can be ordered from:

School Examinations and Assessment Council (SEAC), Newcombe House, Notting Hill Gate, London, W11 3JB; tel: 0171 229-1234; fax: 0171 243-0542.

Index

AAAS (American Association for the Advancement of Science), 134

"above average" scores, 137

accomplishment, levels of
assigning grades to, 123–26
developing for scoring, 116, 117–23
limiting number of, 119

accountability, 3–4

achievement, nonnormative reporting of, 137–38

active assessments, x
appropriate, 136–38
balanced, 85
contextual parameters for, 11–12
cooperative learning, 138
curriculum developers' advice on, 71–85
defined, xii, 1
educational goals and, 132–38
educational values and, 131–39
evaluating effectiveness of, 85
fair, 133–35
guidelines for developing, 84–85
increased, 136
inefficiencies of scoring, 114–15
iterations of, 85
materials, separating from other materials, 56
nonnormative reporting, 137–38
placing within curriculum units, 77–83
political nature of, 131
positive emphasis of, 136
scoring derived from, 111–29
state and national support for, 8–9
teachers' role in, 138
uses of, 71

activity, Dewey's use of term, xii

alternative assessment, xii

ambiguity, lack of, in traditional scoring, 115–16

American Association for the Advancement of Science (AAAS), 134

analytic scoring, 126

aquarium, drawings, 90–91

artistic ability, 88, 136

assessments. See active assessments

assessment strategies, 65–67
assessing individuals in pairs or groups, 65–66
questioning, 67
recording observations, 66

assessment systems, 48–51
building public support for, 67–69
development of, 8–12
explaining to parents, 68–69
for new curriculum projects, 10
transition to, 53–56

assessment tools, 13–51
assessment systems, 48–50
audience-involved, 47
choice of, 13–14
developmental considerations for, 75–77
embedded products and activities, 29–31
multiple-purpose, 55
notebooks and folders, 34–36
observation, 24–25
portfolios, 47–48
postunit assessments, 37–46, 51
prediction activities, 25–29

pre/postunit assessment activities,
14–24
student self-evaluation, 31–33
atomistic scoring, 126
attitudes
assessment of, 83, 84
developing criteria for scoring, 117
expressed in science journals, 107
pre/posttests and, 15
audience-involved assessment, 47
authentic assessment, xii, 7–8
averages, in test scores, 137

Balancing and Weighing, 88
baseline knowledge, measuring with
pretests, 15
"below average" scores, 137
bias
in test content, 133–35
in test structure, 135
Binder, Wendy, 71, 72, 73, 74, 75, 77, 78,
79, 80, 81, 83, 84
biology, structured observation sheets,
94–95
Bones and Skeletons, 35, 36, 40
Boston College, Center for the Study of
Testing, Evaluation, and
Educational Policy, 5
brainstorming
for instruction, 16
pre/postunit, 16–17
Butterflies, 21, 40

California, 9
California, University of, at Los Angeles,
5
California, University of, at Santa
Barbara, 123
California, University of, Lawrence Hall
of Science, 2
Center for Studies in Evaluation (CSE), 5
Center for the Study of Testing,
Evaluation, and Educational Policy,
Boston College, 5
checklists
allowing space for comments, 60–63
including in science notebooks, 58

logistics, 59–62
value of, 59
Chemical Tests, 33, 36, 92
chemistry, pre/postunit assessment,
92–93
children. *See* students
circuses (stations), for postunit assessment, 37–38
class books, 75
class charts, 57
class discussions. *See* conversations;
discussions
colleagues, working with, 54–55, 84–85
concept maps, 23–24
conferences
for assessing work of individuals in
teams, 65
parent-student-teacher, 68–69
Connecticut, 9
constructivism, 7, 132
content
pre/posttests and, 15
testing inequities, 133–35
content-specific tasks and demonstrations, 18
contextual parameters, for assessment,
11–12
conversations. *See also* discussions;
groups
interpretation of, 100–103
as pre-unit assessment, 100–103
supplementing other forms of
assessment with, 99
cooperative learning, xii, 7, 138
criteria
for holistic scoring, 126–27
overdefining, 119
for scoring, 116, 117
CSE (Center for Studies in Evaluation), 5
cultural biases, in standardized tests, 134
curriculum
assessment placement and, 77–83
assessments within units, 79–81
bias in, 134
developmental considerations, 75–77
interpretation of student work and, 83
learning goals and, 73–74, 84

matched assessments and, 77–79
new projects, 10
postunit assessment, 81–83
curriculum developers, assessment and, 71–85
curriculum webs, 23

Daiker, Kathy, 72, 73, 74, 76, 77, 81, 82, 84, 85
data interpretation, as postunit assessment, 39–40
data recording sheets, for prediction activities, 27–29
dating materials
    importance of, 56
    in science notebooks, 57
decontexualization, of traditional testing, 115
demonstrations
    to other students or classrooms, 47
    by teacher, for postunit assessment, 39
developmental considerations, for assessment tools, 75–77
Dewey, John, xii, xiii
dictation, for less-skilled writers, 58
discrimination
    minority groups, 133, 134
    in test content, 133–135
    in test structure, 135
discussions. See also conversations; groups
    as assessment, 65–66, 75–76
    making predictions in, 25
    in matched pre/postunit assessment, 77–78
    for postunit assessments, 81
drawings, 20–23
    in brainstorming for assessment, 17
    developmental considerations, 75
    first-grade aquarium, 90–91
    interpreting, 88–91, 109–110
    for postunit assessments, 81
    scoring, 111
    second-grade physical science, 88
    sixth-grade ecology, 88–89
    value as pre/postunit assessment tool, 20–21

written explanations of, 75

Earth Materials, 76
ecology
    drawings, 88–89
    graphs and tables, 97–100
    notebook entries, 93–94
Ecosystems, 28, 30, 32, 41
EDC. See Education Development Center (EDC)
education
    politics and, 67–68, 131, 132
    social components of, xii
educational reform
    appropriate assessments, 136
    fair assessments, 133–35
    increased assessment, 136
    issues raised by, 133–38
    learning as an active process and, 132
educational values, 131–39
    reflected in active assessments, 136–37
Education Development Center (EDC), 2
    Growing Things, 19, 31, 122–23
    Insights, 10, 40
efficiency, of traditional scoring, 114–15
Electric Circuits, 21, 26–28, 39, 41–44, 48–49, 65
electricity units, embedded assessments, 29–30
embedded assessments, 10, 79
    lessons as, 30–31
    logistics, 57
    products as, 29–30
    teacher's role, 31
embedded lessons, 49
embedded products and activities, 29–31
environmental issues, paper-and-pencil tests, 42–43
equity
    criteria for book and film reviewers, 134
    in test content, 133–35
    in test structure, 135
events, providing reasons for, 58

experiments
    embedded assessments in, 30–31
    hands-on, 40
    interpretation of findings, 39–40
    photographs of, 62
    recording on data collection sheets,
        27–29
    writing conclusions to, 58

fair assessments, 133–35
feelings
    expressed in observations, 88, 90–91
    expressed in science journals, 106–107
first/last lab report/observation, 17–18
Floating and Sinking, 18, 20, 40, 73, 74, 76,
        77, 78, 80, 81
folders
    for assessment, 34–36
    for maintaining materials for assess-
        ment, 56
    for teacher observations, 66
Food Chemistry, 40
FOSS. *See* Full Option Science System
        (FOSS)
Framework for 1994 National Assessment, 137
Full Option Science System (FOSS), 2,
        72, 73
    assessment package, 10
    Earth Materials, 45, 76
    Variables, 41, 45, 46, 72, 74, 82

gender, test scores and, 133
goals
    educational, 132–38
    learning, 73–74, 84
grade inflation, 116
grading. *See also* scoring
    assigning, 123–25
    converting scoring into, 116
    explaining to parents, 68–69
    multiple-choice tests and, 114
    transition to assessment programs, 54
graphs
    interpretation of, 39, 51, 97–100
    sixth-grade ecology, 98–99
    sixth-grade physical science, 97–98
groups. *See also* conversations; discussions
    assessing individual students in,
        65–66, 138

interviews, 66
    valuing, 138
Growing Things, 19, 21, 31, 37–39, 122–23
guests, in classroom, presentations to,
        47

hands-on assessments, 10, 40
    postunit, 82
handwriting, 88
Hartney, David, 72, 73, 74, 76, 77, 78, 80,
        81, 82, 83, 84, 85
higher-order thinking skills, 7
holistic scoring, 126–27
    criteria for, 127
    judgment and, 127

income, test scores and, 133
individual experiments, as postunit
        assessment, 40
inequity
    in test content, 133–35
    in test structure, 135
*Influence of Testing on Teaching Math
        and Science in Grades 4–12*, 5
Insights, 10
    Bones and Skeletons, 35, 36, 40
    Growing Things, 19, 21, 31, 37–39, 122–23
interactive workshops, for explaining
        assessment systems to parents, 68
interpretation of student work, 87–110
    conversations, 100–103
    criteria for, 83, 87
    drawings, 88–91
    examining, 87–88
    graphs and tables, 97–100
    guidelines for, 109–10
    lab reports, 108–109
    science journals, 103–107
    written work, 91–97
interviewing
    groups, 66
    students in pairs, 65–66
    students on teams, 65–66

journals. *See* science journals
judgment
    holistic scoring and, 127
    scoring and, 112–13

Kanevsky, Rhoda, 100
Kids Network, National Geographic, 2
knowledge
　developing criteria for scoring, 117
　language and, ix–x
　revealed in science journals, 107
KWL (Know, Want to know, and
　　Learned) charts, 17, 56

lab procedures, asking students to write,
　58
lab reports
　first/last, 17–18
　interpreting, 108–9
　modeling, 59
lab sheets, 58
language
　interpreting, 110–11
　knowledge and, x
language arts
　assessment changes, 9–10
　emphasis on, 9
　scoring components of, 123–25
learning, xii
　as an active process, 132
　cooperative, 138
　goals, 73–74, 84
　new ideas about, 7–8
learning theory
　constructivist, 132
　multiple-choice tests and, 113–14
lessons, as embedded assessment,
　29–31
levels of accomplishment
　assigning grades to, 123–25
　developing for scoring, 116, 117–23
　limiting, 119
logistics
　checklists, 59–62
　class charts, 57
　guidelines for, 56
　notebooks, 57–59
　photographs, 62
　pre/postunit assessments, 56–57

McDermott, Lillian, 11
Magnets and Motors, 39
managing assessments, 53–69
　assessment strategies, 65–67

logistics, 56–62
public relations, 67–69
transition, 53–56
Massachusetts, MAEP, 8
matched pre/postunit assessment,
　77–79
　class discussions, 77–78
　tasks for, 78–79
measurement tools, for ranking
　schemes, 123
microscope use, embedded assess-
　ments, 30
Minnesota, 9
minority groups, test scores and, 133,
　134
multiple-choice tests, 6, 8. *See also*
　　standardized testing; traditional
　　testing
　assumptions of, 113–14
　children's thinking processes and, 10
　grading and, 114
multiple-purpose assessment tools, 55

NAEP. *See* National Assessment of
　　Educational Progress (NAEP)
National Academy of Science, 8
National Assessment of Educational
　　Progress (NAEP), 4, 8, 116, 137
National Association of School Boards,
　133
National Commission on Excellence in
　　Education, 3
National Committee on Science
　　Education Standards and
　　Assessment, 8
national education goals
　appropriate assessments, 36–38
　assessment and, 132, 133–139
　fair assessments, 133–35
　increased assessments, 136
National Education Goals, 3, 132
National Geographic, Kids Network, 2
National Governors' Association, 3, 132
National Science Foundation, 2
National Science Resources Center
　　(NSRC), 2, 10, 71, 72. *See also*
　　Science and Technology for
　　Children (STC)
National Standards Committee, 8

national testing, support for active
assessment, 8
Nation at Risk, A, 3–4
New York State Department of
Education, 8–9, 136, 137
nonnormative reporting, 137–38
normal distribution curve, achievement
and, 137–38
notebooks, 34–36. *See also* science
notebooks
for assessment, 34–36
for teacher observation, 66
for writing before brainstorming, 16
NSRC. *See* National Science Resources
Center (NSRC)

observation (by teachers)
criteria for, 83
guidelines for, 24–25, 66
observations (by students)
feelings in, 88, 90–91
first/last, 17–18
interpretation of, 93–94
Organisms, 21–23, 40, 41, 72–73, 75, 77,
79, 80, 83, 84

pairs
assessing individual students in,
65–66
interviewing students in, 66
paper-and-pencil tests
evaluating, 43
for postunit assessments, 40–46, 81–82
parents, explaining assessment systems
to, 68–69
parent-student-teacher conferences, for
explaining assessment systems to
parents, 68–69
pedagogic assumptions, of traditional
scoring, 113–14
performance assessments, 7–8, 51
photographs, logistics, 62
physical science
drawings, 88
graphs and tables, 97–98
structured worksheets, 95–97
physical skills, 7
pictorial assessments, 10
postunit, 82, 83

Plant Growth and Development, 27, 50
plant units, embedded assessments,
29–30
politics
assessment system implementation
and, 67–68
education and, 131
scoring changes and, 116
portfolios, 47–48
assessment, of, 7–8, 9
selection of material for, 47–48
positive attitudes, assessment of, 83, 84
positive emphasis, of active assessments, 136
posttests, 14
postunit assessments, 37–46, 49, 51
curriculum and, 81–83
data interpretation, 39–40
demonstrations by teacher, 39
guidelines, 15–16
individual experiments, 40
paper-and-pencil tests, 40–46
pictorial sequencing activities, 51
stations (circuses), 37–38
stories by class or individuals, 40
prediction activities, 25–29
data recording sheets, 27, 29
discussions, 25
prediction activity sheets, 26–27, 49
written predictions, 28–29
preinstruction activities, 14
prelesson assessments, 50
pre/postunit assessment, 14–16
guidelines, 15–16
interpretation of written work,
92–93
logistics, 56–57
matched, 77–79
pre/postunit assessment activities,
14–24
brainstorming, 16–17
concept maps, 23–24
content-specific tasks and demonstrations, 18
drawings, 20–23
first/last lab report/observation,
17–18
observation, 24–25
questionnaires, 19

presentations
  at parents night/open house, 47
  to classroom guests, 47
pretests, 14, 15
preunit assessments, 50
  keeping separate from postunit
    responses, 56–57
products, as embedded assessment,
  29–30
public relations, 67–69
  parents, 68–69
  politics, 67–68

questioning, by teacher, 67
questionnaires, 19

ranking schemes
  development of, 117–23
  guidelines for, 119, 122
reading education, 9
reflection
  asking questions inspiring, 58
  in portfolio material selection,
    47–48
reflective assessments, 10
  postunit, 82, 83
rehearsals, for public presentations,
  47
reliability, of traditional scoring, 115
repetition, as opportunity for assessment, 80–81

school budgets, cuts in, 4
Schools Examinations and Assessment
  Council, 113
Science Books & Films, 134
science education, ix
  accountability and, 3–4
  active student participation, 6
  changes in, 6–7
  content areas of, scoring and, 117
  emphasis on, 1–2
  equity criteria for books and films, 134
  objectives of, 6–7
  reform, xi, 3
  spending on, 2–3
science folders. See folders
Science Framework (1994), 8, 137
science journals

attitudes expressed in, 107
comparing early and later entries,
  106–107, 109
feelings expressed in, 107
interpretation of, 103–107
introducing, 54
knowledge revealed in, 107
science skills revealed in, 107
science notebooks
  for assessment, 34–36
  conversion of entries into numerical
    scores, 123–25
  copying questions into, 58
  guidelines for keeping, 57–59
  helping students understand reasons
    for keeping, 59
  interpretation of work, 93–94
  logistics, 57–59
  organizing, 58
  vs. portfolios, 47–48
  reading and commenting in, 59
Science and Technology for Children
  (STC), 2, 26, 27, 28, 72
  assessment system, 10
  Balancing and Weighing, 88
  brainstorming examples, 16
  Butterflies, 21, 39, 40
  Chemical Tests, 33, 36, 92
  Ecosystems, 28, 32, 41
  Electric Circuits, 21, 26–28, 39, 41,
    42–44, 48–49, 65
  Floating and Sinking, 18, 20, 40, 73, 74,
    76, 77, 78, 80, 81
  Food Chemistry, 40
  Organisms, 21–23, 40, 41, 72–73, 75, 77,
    79, 80, 83, 84
  Plant Growth and Development, 27, 50
scientific concepts, developmental
  considerations, 76
scientific method, 7
scientific skills, developmental considerations, 76
scoring, 111–29. See also grading;
  traditional scoring
  active assessments, 116–27
  analytic, 126
  assigning grades to levels of accom-
    plishment, 123–25
  atomistic, 126

converting into grades, 116
derived from assessments, 112–13, 116–29
determining levels of accomplishment, 116, 117–23
developing criteria for, 116, 117
holistic, 126–27
judgment involved in, 112–13
need for, 111–12
nonnormative reporting and, 137–38
ranking schemes, 117–23
rubrics, 117–23
traditional, 113–16
uses of, 112–13
value of, 129
self-evaluation, by students, 31–33, 65, 78
short-answer tests, children's thinking processes and, 10
skills
developing criteria for scoring, 117
pre/posttests and, 15
revealed in science journals, 107
small groups. See also groups
assessing individual students in, 65–66
speculation, questions inspiring, 58
spelling, 88
standardized tests. See also multiple-choice tests; traditional scoring; traditional testing
inadequacy of, 4–5
inequity in, 133–35
interpretation of, 115–16
lack of teacher involvement in, 138
state testing, support for active assessment, 8–9
Statewide Systemic Initiative (SSI), 2
stations (circuses), for postunit assessment, 37–38
STC. See Science and Technology for Children (STC)
stories, class/individual, as postunit assessment, 40
structural inequity, in testing, 135
structured observation sheets, interpretation of, 94–95

structured worksheets, interpretation of, 95–97
students
criteria for interpreting work of, 83
interpreting work of, 87–110
participation by, 6
photographing activities of, 62
self-evaluation by, 31–33, 65, 78
teaching by, 47
thinking processes, research studies, 10–11

tables
interpreting, 97–100
sixth-grade ecology, 98–100
sixth-grade physical science, 97–98
tasks, for matched pre/postunit assessment, 78–79
teachers, role in assessment, 138
teaching, by students, 47
teams, assessing individual students in, 65–66
testing, traditional. See traditional testing
thinking skills, 7
traditional scoring, 113–16. See also standardized tests; traditional testing
efficiency of, 114–15
interpretation of, 115–16
pedagogic assumptions of, 113–14
policy changes and, 116
reliability, 115
reputed strengths of, 114–16
unambiguousness of, 115–16
traditional testing, 1. See also standardized tests
assumptions of, 113–14
decontextualization of, 115
equity and, xii, 133–35
inadequacy of, 4–5, 6–7, 11
limitations of, ix
political issues, xi
transition to assessment programs, 53–56

UCLA, Center for Studies in Evaluation (CSE), 5

values
    educational, 131–39
    reflected in active assessments,
        136–37
Variables, 41, 45, 46, 72, 74, 82

weather unit, embedded assessments,
    30
whole language education, 9–10
word use, interpreting, 109
workload, managing, during transition
    to assessment programs, 55
writing
    about team activities, 65
    allowing adequate time for, 58
    alternatives to, 59
    before brainstorming, 16
    dictation, 58
    existing programs, science notebooks
        and, 54

written assessments, appropriateness
    of, 75
written predictions, 28–29
written work
    fourth-grade chemistry pre/postunit
        assessment, 92–93
    interpretation of, 91–97
    sixth-grade biology structured
        observation sheets, 94–95
    sixth-grade notebook entries on
        ecology, 93–94
    sixth-grade physical science struc-
        tured worksheets, 95–97

young children, developmental consid-
    erations in assessing, 75–76